The Theatre Student:

ON STAGE:
PRODUCING MUSICAL THEATRE

by

Gerald Lee Ratliff

and

Suzanne Trauth

THE ROSEN PUBLISHING GROUP, INC.

NEW YORK

Published in 1988 by The Rosen Publishing Group
29 East 21st Street, New York, New York 10010

First Edition
Copyright 1988 by Gerald Lee Ratliff and Suzanne Trauth

Library of Congress Cataloging-in-Publication Data

Ratliff, Gerald Lee.
    On stage.

    (The Theatre student)
    Bibliography: p.
    Includes index.
    1. Musical revue, comedy, etc.—Production
and direction. I. Trauth, Suzanne.   II. Title.
II. Series.
MT955.R37   1988   782.81′07′1   86-20325
ISBN 0-8239-0697-3

Manufactured in the United States of America

ACKNOWLEDGMENTS

One of the truly remarkable and rewarding experiences of the past five years has been my association with the Rosen Press, especially the caring and devoted support of Ruth Rosen and her family and friends. The many exciting projects I have helped to shape and frame are the result of the special relationship I have enjoyed with these visionary compatriots! For all the hours and months spent on this project, I should like to thank my wonderful and wise co-author, Suzanne Trauth, who constantly provides the inspiration and comfort needed to sustain creative thought; my many colleagues who supplied photographs and ideas to finalize the project; and my special family of rooters: Richard, Myrtle, Larry, Ann, Frank, Donna, and Peggy.

Gerald Lee Ratliff

The writing of this text has been a learning experience in itself. Without the cooperation and encouragement of many people, it would have been impossible to see it through to completion. I am grateful to all of the actors with whom I have ever worked—they've taught me that directing is a quest for creativity and a wonderful opportunity to communicate to many people on a very special level; to Bill Brewer for having made musical production fun; to my students who, in questioning the theatrical process, keep me always on my toes; to the cast and crew of *The Boy Friend* for providing inspiration at the right moments; to my colleague Gerald Lee Ratliff for his constant enthusiasm, generosity, and sense of humor; and, finally, to Elaine Insinnia, whose patience, support, and suggestions regarding this manuscript have made the project possible.

Suzanne Trauth

ABOUT THE AUTHORS

Gerald Lee Ratliff is Associate Professor and Chairman of the Department of Speech and Theatre at Montclair State College, Upper Montclair, New Jersey. Among other professional activities, he is past president of the Speech and Theatre Association of New Jersey and the School Senate of Fine and Performing Arts, editor of the national theatre journals *Secondary School Theatre Journal* and *The Cue*, and on the editorial board of *Reader's Theatre News* and the *Liberal and Fine Arts Review.*

Dr. Ratliff is the author of numerous essays and articles for scholarly periodicals on the topics of Bertolt Brecht, reader's theatre, performance studies, and literary criticism including publications in *Theatre Journal, Professional Communication, National Forum, Issues in Interpretation, College English Notes, Gestus, Theatre News, School Arts, College Literature,* and the *Eugene O'Neill Newsletter.* His most recent project in literary criticism was the critical analysis and interpretation notes of *Oedipus the King* and *The Prince* for Barron's Educational Series.

Suzanne Trauth is an Assistant Professor of Theatre, Managing Director of the Major Theatre Series, and Chair of the Theatre Division of the Department of Speech and Theatre, Montclair State College, Upper Montclair, New Jersey. She has directed and produced musicals and opera, as well as nonmusical productions, in a variety of settings including several Off-Broadway theatres in New York City. In addition to her creative work as director and producer, Dr. Trauth has served on the Legislative Council and as Secretary of the Theatre Division of the Speech Communication Association.

Dr. Trauth has authored papers for such journals as *Empirical Research in Theatre, Association for Communication Administration Bulletin,* the *Kansas Speech Journal,* and *Cue,* the journal of Theta Alpha Phi, a national theatre honorary society. Recently, she published an article on Antoinette Perry in *Notable Women in the American Theatre.* She has presented papers at a variety of national and state speech and theatre associations including the American Theatre Association, the Speech Communication Association, and the East Central Theatre Conference.

CONTENTS

TO THE INSTRUCTOR

This book is designed to suggest to you possible avenues of approach to the exciting activity of presenting a musical. It endeavors to clarify problems you might encounter when producing or directing a musical and suggests simple and practical performance and production methods in the process of staging. The authors also provide creative exercises to assist your students in preparing for the musical production.

The book is organized into a general historical overview of the elements of the musical; performance models for acting in the musical; practical suggestions for directing the musical and staging choreography; and imaginative management principles and techniques to publicize a production. No attempt is made to categorize which approaches to the topics are "best"; a variety of suggestions are made that offer alternative approaches. You, of course, are always at liberty to supplement the theory and activities described and to incorporate your own performance and production approaches to meet the special demands of your students.

In using the book for classroom or public performance and production, you are encouraged to establish a clear set of objectives for each chapter and to be flexible in approach so that your students may experiment and explore freely without a preconceived system of discoveries or finalities guiding the response. The key word is adaptability; you should relate the theory and the exercises to the skills of your students. Cultivate the attitude that musical theatre is an arena for serious and disciplined study, and that careful review of the principles of performance and production helps to promote a polished and professional product.

Use of the exercises in the book should help your students achieve more self-discipline and satisfaction in their ability to perform in front of an audience. Be sure to set aside ample class or rehearsal time for the vocal and physical warm-ups, and consult the bibliography for references and sources of information related to choreography/movement, scenery/costumes, lighting/sound, and directing/producing. The appendix provides lists of rental agencies for musicals and of both popular musicals and recent musicals that you might wish to consider for production.

As you begin reading the individual chapters that comprise the book, remember that the focus is on the learning process. The learning skills described are intended to help your students gain confidence in their personal development, and any artistic or critical evaluation of a student's performance should serve only to promote growth and creativity. Above all, encourage your students to continually educate themselves by watching other musical performers, observing daily life for potential character portraits, and becoming more receptive to constructive criticism and more disciplined and determined in rehearsal and performances.

In using the supplementary exercises, have a clear set of objectives in mind but be flexible so that your students may explore freely. Insist on sufficient preparation and home study, perhaps supplemented by library research and written evaluations, to promote a more informed study of the musical. Cultivate the positive attitude that the successful performance and production of musicals is a daily matter of keen observation, studied investigation, and creative experimentation. The wider the range of experience and example from which acting, directing, or producing the musical can be studied, the more likely it is that the performance and the production will be inspired.

TO THE STUDENT

You are embarking on a great adventure! The study and performance of musical theatre offers the actor, director, and producer one of the richest theatrical experiences possible. The combination of music, dance, and script will provide challenges and opportunities for stretching your imagination and expanding your sense of self and of production physically, emotionally, and psychologically. Because musical theatre artists rely heavily on sound and movement, as well as the spoken word, they touch audiences in a very special, human, universal manner. It is quite a responsibility.

This book is intended as a travel guide as you begin your musical journal. Our hope is to provide you with ideas and options that will broaden your vision of this truly unique theatrical form. There is no right way or wrong way to perform or direct or produce a musical production. There are only ways that are more productive, more creative, more interesting, and, ultimately, more enjoyable. We hope to present some techniques, practical hints, and points of view that will help you find the most productive approach for *you*. Creating any work of art is an individualistic process, and it is important that you identify the procedures that best locate the key to your creative imagination.

Begin your study of the musical by reading Part I. It provides an overview of the structure of musicals: how plot, characterization, and dialogue contribute to a well-formed piece of comedy or drama. Understanding the history of the musical permits you to evaluate contemporary productions better. They have not been created in isolation, but rather are the products of a long, detailed process of evolution. Numerous examples support the discussion of structure and performance approach to musical theatre.

The detailed exercises on breath support, vocal mechanics, body flexibility, and communication are designed to provide you with tools to train your voice and body. Musical theatre performance is a demanding experience for any actor, and it is especially difficult if the instrument, you, is not well-trained. The type of exercises included require commitment and dedication. One cannot correct faulty breathing patterns or a lack of body expressiveness overnight. Such problems demand daily attention, the kind of attention you would give any activity that was especially meaningful for you. If you are a serious performer and intend to pursue your study of musical theatre in the future, it is wise to begin to discipline yourself now. Part II of this book should help you create a personal approach to training your instrument.

For those who are more interested in directing or are curious about the relationship between the director and the actors during rehearsal of a musical, Part III introduces the various tasks undertaken by the director in the course of the production: choosing a musical, casting, script and character analyses, and working with the other members of the production team—choreographer, musical director, and designers. For an actor it is helpful to understand the directing process in order to collaborate creatively with the director. Knowing what the director expects from you and how your character is part of the director's vision of the show can only contribute positively to your growth as an actor.

Part IV is for those with a business bent or managerial skills. You may not have the opportunity to produce a full musical production at this time, but if the business end of theatre appeals to you, you might consider producing as a future activity. The description of the producer's job outlines the primary areas of concern: creating the budget and managing the fiscal affairs of the show, overseeing the operation of the box office, and managing publicity and promotion activities. Producing is a demanding and difficult task, but one that is ultimately rewarding.

Finally, we have prepared an extensive bibliography and lists of musicals for future reference as you work both in the classroom setting and on the stage. All of the basic information that you might require as you begin your study of the musical theatre is provided for you here. All you need do is jump in! Absorb the history, experiment with the exercises, explore the approaches, read widely, and, most important, have fun. Your experiences with musical theatre may be the most exciting events in your theatrical life.

Part I

PRELUDE
TO THE
MUSICAL THEATRE

PRELUDE TO THE MUSICAL THEATRE

For the past fifty years musical theatre has been the most popular form of live entertainment in America. Most people refer to it as "musical comedy," but such recent examples as *Sweeney Todd, Sunday in the Park with George,* and *Cats* contain such intense emotion, thought, and depth of characterization that musical theatre should be thought of as more than comedy.

The early roots of musical theatre are found in the sentimental Viennese operetta, the satirical Parisian comic opera, the vaudeville revue, British slapstick burlesque skits and pantomimes, and music hall recitals. Until recently, serious critics of the theatre tended to deprecate the musical as "sound and fury, signifying nothing." Finally, however, even they have begun to recognize the artistic achievement that is possible in musical theatre when story, characters, music, dance, and spectacle are imaginatively integrated into a production that is not only full of dash and energy but also thought-provoking and intellectually stimulating.

An integral feature of the musical is that the songs and dances grow out of the plot and the characters express themselves lyrically rather than in prose dialogue. For example, when Eliza Doolittle in *My Fair Lady* has at last learned to pronounce her vowels correctly, she musically transforms her prose sentences about "the rain in Spain" into an energetic tango and celebrates her accomplishment in a song that captures her excitement at having pleased her teacher, Henry Higgins.

Between the individual songs of the major characters, the musical is shaped by elaborate production numbers at the beginning, in the middle, and at the end. There are supporting choruses of singers in bright costumes, crowds of dancers in picturesque formations, colorful lighting, and imaginative scene changes that captivate the viewing audience. Such spectacle may be a pleasure in itself,

as it is in the bright and engaging production of *Forty-Second Street*, but it can also create a social and geographical backdrop against which to develop the main story. For example, in *South Pacific*, when you weave together "There Is Nothing Like a Dame" for the lovelorn American Seabees, "Bloody Mary" for the lusty madam, "Bali Hai" for the exotic native girls, and "Dites moi" for the French planter's children, you have the social and geographical exposition that helps to explain in song the sad love of Lieutenant Cable for the beautiful Nellie Forbush.

Ever since the first "true American musical," *The Black Crook* (1866), dance has been as important as music in helping to visualize the storyline of a musical theatre script. For a long time, however, dance in musical theatre consisted of well-drilled lines of brightly costumed chorus girls stepping, kicking, and whirling as they faced the audience. With the emergence of creative choreographers trained in both ballet and modern dance techniques, musical theatre dance has become an integral part of the plot and is frequently used, as in *Cabaret,* to help define character thoughts and emotions. The first significant appearance of dance in musical theatre was the ballet choreography created by Agnes de Mille in the 1943 production of *Oklahoma!*

Although there was imaginative dance throughout the production of *Oklahoma!*, the visual high point was the "dream ballet." Laurey's groundless fears that she may have been too harsh with Curly and too romantically involved with the dangerous Jud were acted out in an exceptionally well-executed ballet. The characters gave expression to their fears, emotions, and hopes in an orchestrated sequence of movement, spacing, lighting, and character relationship spelled out in ballet. An even closer integration of dance and storyline was seen in the

The close integration of dance and storyline is clearly evident in the popular theatrical celebration *A CHORUS LINE*, Broadway's longest running musical. (From the Berea Summer Theatre (Ohio) production. Directed by William Allman and Conley Schaterbeck.)

1957 production of *West Side Story*, especially the "rumble sequence," and in the more recent *A Chorus Line*, Broadway's longest-running musical. All of these productions highlight the easy blending of dance and dialogue and provide models of audience expectations when viewing a musical.

The general characteristics of American musical comedy have evolved significantly from the early 1940s to the present day. Audience expectations have changed little in that continuing development, and the commercial success or failure of new musicals may depend on their ability to strike a responsive and familiar chord of audience approval based upon the following criteria.

I. *CHARACTERS:* Many characters in musicals are based on stereotypes, the most common being young lovers, heroes, heroines, villains, and simple folk. The general classifications are ingenue, juvenile, leading man, leading woman, character man, character woman, and exotic.

II. *VALUES:* Most values are related to overcoming obstacles, being reunited with a lost love, changing social views, winning a dispute, and offering an alternative to the usual way of viewing a problem.

III. *LANGUAGE:* Characters speak prose in simple, direct exclamations that quickly move the story to the next song. The short dialogue is interspersed with recitative and lyrical song, either solo or group. Songs are voiced in complicated rhymes and intricate rhythms that help to suggest the mood or attitude of the character.

IV. *MOVEMENT:* Movement is agile and believable when executed in nonsinging scenes and helps to establish and refine character relationships. In nonspeaking scenes, movement is aggressive and extreme, with complex dance combinations of tap, jazz, modern, and ballet to enhance the pacing of the story or to highlight the emotional mood or attitude of the characters.

V. *SPECTACLE:* Spectacle is the ultimate tool of visualization. Every possible type of hand prop—umbrella, gun, walking stick, luggage, handbag, and briefcase—is used to provide active stage business. Scenery that flies, glides, and turns is essential for the many transformations and changes of scene that are required. Costume changes are also frequent, and the emphasis is on bright hues and glittering fabrics. The most recent element of spectacle is the elaborate use of slides, projections, and film sequences as backdrops.

The audience expectations described above pose real problems for musical theatre performers. For example, they need a strong singing voice, extensive dance training, especially in tap and jazz, gymnastic ability for tumbling, falling, and fighting, a flair for comedic delivery of lines, ability to read music, special skills in circus techniques, improvi-

sation, and magic, physical and vocal flexibility, a vibrant personality or charisma that projects across the footlights, and an intense dedication to the musical theatre profession at a time when few plays are commercial successes.

To make clearer the unique elements of musical theatre in both performance and production, let us review the general characteristics and technical demands of subject matter, style, artistic form, and structure.

THE LIBRETTO

The libretto of a musical comprises the words or text of spoken dialogue and the lyrics of the songs. It is an elaborate scenario, or outline, of the sequence of songs, dialogue, dances, and reprises that create the spirit and the atmosphere of the musical.

Like the musical interpretation of a printed score, the libretto frequently depends upon the director's and actors' creative ability to envision a performance solely from words, songs, and actions. Understanding the basic ingredients of the musical theatre script should give you the critical skills necessary to visualize a potential production. Such an approach demands a responsive mind that is capable of capturing and cataloguing a flurry of vivid and relevant speeches, songs, images, and actions. Here are some interpretative principles to guide you in adapting the read libretto to the imaginative stage of your own mind.

- Read the preface or introduction to the musical, familiarizing yourself with any critical commentary that precedes the printed book or score. Of particular value would be discussion of the author's dramatic techniques, or the historical period of the musical.
- Pay attention to the title of the musical. Titles often suggest the author's point of view or indicate the thematic approach necessary for understanding. For example, the title *Cats* might suggest that the action is concerned with feline or catlike images related to being crafty, sly, or stealthy.
- Review the character names to find possible characterization *approaches*. For example,

the character Sky Masterson in *Guys and Dolls* is a professional gambler with "heavenly aspirations"; the character "The Red Shadow" in *The Desert Song* is a disguised Robin Hood, fearless and heroic in his efforts to right wrongs.

- Be aware of the description of character in the libretto, especially revealed in individual songs to express emotion, mood, or attitude. Character evaluation may help you to discover the author's approach to human nature, and may also reveal the motivation that leads a character to perform specific actions. For example, Billy Bigelow in *Carousel* is a drunkard and a bum who refuses to support his wife until he discovers that she is pregnant. His belated reversal is both desperate and disastrous, and he resorts to robbery and, finally, suicide.

- Critically chart the actions of a character from the first entrance to the last exit. Actions help to mirror and reflect character thought or attitude and to reveal why a character speaks or sings in a particular way at a particular moment.

- Read the musical as you might read a short story, sorting out the character relationships and allowing the story to tell itself in both the dialogue and the songs. Try to read it in one sitting, noting the momentum of the action and the character development. Note the description of the setting and the needed props, costumes, or other theatrical devices.

- Critically chart the songs and the dances, and note the changing mood and tempo of your character. You should be able to sense both the type and the style of songs and dances, whether it be a romantic ballad or a comic narrative, a jazz or a modern dance technique.

- Reread the libretto for clarity and comprehension, paying special attention to subtle nuances of meaning suggested by the dialogue or the lyrics. Reevaluate the primary scenes of confrontation or disagreement between characters, and try to visualize their conflicting attitudes and responses. Rethink your initial interpretation of the author's point of view, and then isolate those specific lines of dialogue or lyrics that help to reinforce and amplify your interpretation.

THE PLOT

The plot, or storyline, of musicals is often quite different from the traditional theatre playscript. The most obvious difference is the absence of description, narration, and detail that the theatre playscript employs to "flesh out" the storyline and the development of character. There are also fewer complications, reversals, and recognition scenes to delineate or clarify character moods and attitudes. In addition, the plot of musicals frequently has the following general characteristics that distinguish it from the traditional theatre storyline:

- The opening scene of musicals introduces the principal character(s) and establishes the inherent conflict of personality or thought that must be resolved in the later development of the plot.

- The storyline is primarily simple and highlights individual or ensemble songs rather than complicated exchanges of dialogue.

- Dialogue and lyrics are clear and precise and rely on images to convey the thought, mood, or emotion of the moment.

- The plot is embellished by elaborate ensemble songs, reprises, and dances that frame the main action of the characters.

- Musicals inherently underplay the psychological or intellectual exploration of character development and concentrate primarily on expressing the emotional content of a character's mood or attitude.

An analogy or comparison can be drawn between the plot structure of a musical and the architectural design of a building. Both the musical author and the architect plan a foundation, whether of songs and dialogue or concrete, that will support the proposed structure; and both calculate the dimensions, size, and scope that will give the musical or the building its inner strength and outer beauty.

The typical musical plot structure includes *exposition, complication,* and *resolution.*

Exposition, which gives the background information needed by the viewer to understand the character relationships or actions, generally occurs briefly in the first scene of a musical and may be referred to as an ''introduction'' to the storyline. For example, in *The King and I* we learn early that the arrogant King of Siam has sent for a Welsh schoolmistress, Anna, to educate his numerous children and wives. This brief exposition serves to propel the plot of the musical to its happy conclusion, Anna's teaching the King how to be humble and graceful.

Complication, the real or imagined obstacles that create conflict and bar a character from realizing his or her objectives, generally occurs midway in the musical and provides character development. In *West Side Story,* for example, we learn that Tony and Maria are hopelessly in love but cannot overcome the obstacle of a street society that is violent and irreconcilable in its differences.

Resolution, which details how previous actions, situations, and character relationships are finally concluded, generally occurs toward the last half of the musical and may be seen as a precise summary of the conflict developed in the complication. In *Gypsy,* for example, we learn that an ambition-driven mother, Rose, almost drives both of her daughters to despair by her persistent interference in their lives, only to become aware in the resolution that her daughters need freedom to make their own decisions.

Although the plot structure of musicals varies according to the style and intent of the author, the pattern of shape, form, and meaning inherent in each musical provides ample opportunity for experimentation. For example, the musicals *Working* and *Company* are mosaics of individual plots that revolve around a major character or a primary theme; and *Sweeney Todd* is a rich tapestry of murder and mayhem not generally thought of as a suitable plot for a musical comedy.

As you become more familiar with the plot structure of musicals, remember that the author has consciously arranged each scene and song for a specific purpose, and that each scene and song logically and organically should evolve from what has preceded it. Like the cub reporter, approach a study of musical plot structure by asking *who, what, when, where,* and *why.* What should emerge from your study is a pattern of construction that reveals thoughts or ideas presented through song or dialogue, and characters and actions that are ultimate expressions of the author's point of view.

THE CHARACTERS

Characterizations in musicals should paint lifelike portraits of persons drawn from the workaday world. However, authors of musicals often rely primarily on stereotypical figures that are easily identified by their attitude, neurosis, behavior, or point of view. Some of the most common stereotypical musical characters are the following:

- romantic hero (Sky Masterson in *Guys and Dolls*)
- comic con artist (Bloody Mary in *South Pacific*)
- daring villain (Ludwig in *Pal Joey*)
- nonconformist (Tevye in *Fiddler on the Roof*)
- sophisticated lady (Vera in *Pal Joey*)
- innocent heroine (Laurey in *Oklahoma!*)
- star-crossed lovers (Tony and Maria in *West Side Story*)
- comic old man (Major General in *The Pirates of Penzance*)
- threatening antagonist (Jud in *Oklahoma!*)
- domineering mother (Rose in *Gypsy*)
- wise confidant (Col. Pickering in *My Fair Lady*)

Although characters sometimes appear superficial—using costumes, props, and scenic devices to communicate changing attitudes and moods—an attempt is still made to present vivid, incisive por-

Although there is every attempt to paint lifelike portraits of recognizable persons in musicals, some musical theatre characters are so vivid and incisive that they mirror reality. The comic con artist in *OLIVER!*, for example, engages in ignorant blunders and exhibits both courage and cowardice in displaying basic emotional urges. (From the production of Murray State University. Directed by Mark Malinauskas; designed by Karen Boyd; and choreographed by Beverly Rogers.)

traits that mirror reality. As a consequence, we hear—in both dialogue and song—characters performing heroic deeds, making ignorant blunders, exhibiting both courage and cowardice, committing errors in judgment, or displaying basic emotions such as anger, frustration, and greed.

Characters also reflect the environmental, psychological, and emotional forces that have helped shape their present circumstances. They deal with issues of a social, political, or moral nature and take significant action against forces that appear to limit their chances for survival and success. In addition, characters possess admirable values, principles, and morals: especially those "heroic" figures who speak or sing directly and sincerely about the truth of their lives.

An interesting aspect of recent musicals such as *The Best Little Whorehouse in Texas*, *Pippin*, *The Robber Bridegroom*, and *Jesus Christ, Superstar* is an honest attempt to portray accurately the facts of contemporary life. Approaching everyday existence with a keen and objective eye, these musicals are concerned with advancing social changes, reinforcing standard values, or encouraging new interpretations of old religious, political, social, or moral issues. Surface details, common actions, and the minor catastrophes of a middle-class society also comprise the subject matter of some recent musicals—*Chicago*, *Sweeney Todd*, and *Barnum*—and provide the sometimes grim backdrop against which the truth of human sympathy and compassion is explored.

The characters of musicals usually find themselves in unfortunate yet comic situations that afford no convenient means of escape. Yet they endure hardship and encounter rejection and hostility with the hope and determination that prove their true value. The potentially tragic circumstances these characters face—losing a job, being broke, doing work not suited to their talents, or dreaming of a better life-style—are invariably resolved through their own ingenuity; but they exhibit in their strength of character the ability to transcend the immediate consequences of their plight and to achieve a measure of personal dignity and distinc-

tion. They are at their most exalted in singing the songs that communicate their frustration or underscore their optimism for the future. The following song titles are representative of the nature of musical characters confronting almost insurmountable odds with courage and determination:

- "Anything You Can Do" (*Annie Get Your Gun*)
- "One of a Kind" (*Applause*)
- "Put on a Happy Face" (*Bye Bye Birdie*)
- "Live and Let Live" (*Can-Can*)
- "The Best of All Possible Worlds" (*Candide*)
- "You Musn't Be Discouraged" (*Fade-Out Fade-In*)
- "People" (*Funny Girl*)
- "I Got Life" (*Hair*)
- "Nobody's Perfect" (*I Do! I Do!*)
- "If I Had My Druthers" (*Li'l Abner*)
- "The Impossible Dream" (*Man of La Mancha*)
- "Without You I'm Nothing" (*Mr. Wonderful*)
- "I Won't Grow Up" (*Peter Pan*)
- "He Can Do It" (*Purlie*)
- "I Ain't Down Yet" (*The Unsinkable Molly Brown*)
- "Happiness" (*You're a Good Man, Charlie Brown*)

By paying attention to the songs of the musical, you should notice that characters emerge stronger from facing the obstacles they see as limiting their potential success. Another clue can be gained from observing the pattern of suffering and despair so common in musicals: Look for the honesty and frankness in the songs of your character and note how the lyrics help to reflect his or her basic nature and disposition. This approach should help you to understand more fully the issue being presented by the author.

THE TIME AND THE ACTION

The passage of time and continuous action in the musical quickly elapse between the scenes or acts. Unlike the chronological structure of the typical theatre script, the musical compresses time and action into an immediacy that suggests momentum and suspense. For example, several months elapse between Act I and Act II of *My Fair Lady* as Eliza learns to speak correctly; fifteen years elapse in Act II, scenes three and four, of *Carousel* to permit Billy's daughter to grow to adolescence; and more than ten years elapse in *Jesus Christ, Superstar* to account for the events of the Old Testament story.

Suspending both time and action permits the musical to detail a series of apparently unrelated events, or to underscore several events simultaneously. The arrangement of scenes and acts is then concerned with a description of events in the present tense, and there are occasionally repetitions of events or activities that imply a duplication of previous episodes. The suspension of time and action in a carefully structured, chronological fashion further encourages the viewer to supply the background information necessary to understand the characters and the action.

Perhaps this approach to structure accounts for the sometimes superficial or one-dimensional nature of character motivation and subsequent action. It could also account for characterization that is simplistic in its expression of impulses and desires. In spite of the apparent lack of character development when time and action are suspended, however, the brevity of scenes and the urgent nature of the "present tense" help to sharpen the viewer's perception and arouse deeper emotions because of the immediate and objective treatment.

LIGHTING

The role of special lighting effects in musicals continues to grow in importance as sophisticated productions like *Cats, A Chorus Line, 42nd Street,* and *Sunday in the Park with George* add new technical demands to staging. As musical scripts rely less and less on plot development and characterization to delineate the storyline, lighting has begun to bespeak the mood, to define character relationships, to provide spatial contrast, and to highlight significant scenes.

Of all lighting instruments, the spotlights appears to be the ideal friend of the musical. Spotlights help to focus audience attention on significant scenes, isolate the action, highlight the leading performers, and create a mood. It is still customary to bathe solo and duet singers in spotlights and to blanket the stage in multicolored light for elaborate dance sequences. Notice the role that lighting plays in conveying character mood and attitude the next time you see a musical, and pay special attention to the subtle changes in color, intensity, and focus as you observe changing character relationships and the author's subtle point of view.

If you are familiar with the technical aspects of theatre lighting, you know that illumination of the downstage area from the beam position is not common in the commercial theatre, especially the Broadway playhouses of New York City. The most common practice is to focus spotlights hung from frames on the front of the upper balcony, or to place partly concealed spots in boxes on the side walls of the auditorium. The front of the balcony places the spotlight at a much lower angle than the beam position and highlights the face in a complimentary fashion.

The effective lighting of a musical, therefore, depends upon a proper mixture of "general" and "specific" lighting effects. General illumination softens shade and shadow, modifies excessive contrasts in specific illumination, and creates the general color tonality of the entire stage. Specific illumination reveals form, highlights individual areas of the stage, and helps to focus viewer attention on the action.

Lighting is also the principal means of illuminating the background elements of the stage design, primarily the cyclorama and the painted drop. Lights focused on the cyclorama—a large canvas curtain hung from a horizontal U-shaped frame suspended by sets of lines from the gridiron—and the painted drop provide the environment of the musical scene and help to emphasize the action of the moment.

The effective lighting of a musical depends upon a proportioned mixture of both ''general'' and ''specific'' lighting effects. Lighting also helps to focus viewer attention on the action being presented. In the musical adaptation of *THE SECOND SHEPHERD'S PLAY*, for example, lighting highlights the emotional mood of the scene and helps to emphasize the specific action of the moment. (From the production of Southern Seminary Junior College. Directed and designed by William Rough. Photography by Patrick Hinely. Choreography by Carol Kirgis.)

Look carefully at the role lighting plays in the next musical you attend. Does the lighting help create the mood of the book? Is it possible to detect the ''moments'' being highlighted by spotlights? Does the lighting convey a pleasing tonality to the stage set without detracting from the performance? Those are questions you should pose in your critical observation of lighting in musicals.

Cyclorama

Wings   *Wings*

Upstage

Left   Right

Downstage

3   2   1   3   2   1

Curtain Line

SPECIAL CONSIDERATIONS

Musical theatre stagecraft has its own terminology. Review the diagram to familiarize yourself with a typical musical production.

Stage right and stage left are always determined from the actor's position as he faces the audience.

Downstage is toward the audience; upstage, away from the audience. Other primary areas are down center and up center; down right and down left, the two downstage corners closest to the audience; and up right and up left, the two upstage corners farthest from the audience. All of the stage positions have shorthand abbreviations:

SR: Stage Right	SL: Stage Left
DS: Down Stage	US: Up Stage
DC: Down Center	UC: Up Center
DR: Down Right	DL: Down Left
UR: Up Right	UL: Up Left

The cyclorama is a large curved curtain that surrounds the upstage area of the performance space. It is sometimes painted if it is used throughout the musical, but usually it is used to block off the backstage area or to serve as a screen for projections of the sky, the sea, or a landscape needed to detail the locale of a scene.

The wings, on each side of the stage, are counted from downstage to upstage and are marked off by high, narrow curtains called *legs*. Sometimes, wings are painted stage flats that help to block off backstage areas. Wings are especially important in musical productions because of large group entrances and exits from the sides of the stage.

RHYTHM AND RANGE

The two basic tempos of the musical are double and triple, or 2/4 and 3/4 time. The 2/4 time, called "up tempo," is fast and lively. Based upon two beats to the bar, 2/4 time is the most rhythmic. A good example is "Why Can't the English" from *My Fair Lady.*

The 3/4 time is "waltz" rhythm and is flowing and light. It has three beats to the measure and varies the degree of emphasis on the first accent. An example is "Someone Is Waiting" from *Company.*

Although the human voice has the narrowest range of any instrument, it has the most shades and tones of vocal coloring and is capable of producing imaginative effects. The voice has four primary registers, and they fall into the following ranges:

Soprano:	Middle C to A below High C
Alto:	G below Middle C to C above Middle C
Bass:	G twice below Middle C to Middle C
Tenor:	C below Middle C to A above Middle C
Baritone:	A twice below Middle C to E above Middle C

The usual professional range within any vocal register is twelve notes, or an octave and a half. Few musical theatre songs exceed a ten-note range, so the performer must frequently rely upon coloring and shading to give the voice dimension.

Your approach to both rhythm and range should be under the careful guidance of a professional musical coach. Your coaching should include correct breathing techniques, development of a vibrant timbre color, vocal harmony, and training in solo, duet, trio, and ensemble numbers. It should explore the proper techniques for producing resonance in the head ("head voice") and in the chest ("chest voice").

MELODY

Melody in musicals can be explored by reviewing the traditional meter of a show tune: the scheme of AABA:

A: Initial statement of the melody.

A: Repetition of the intitial statement of the melody.

B: Contrast or opposite statement of the melody (commonly termed a "break" or a "bridge").

A: Repetition of the initial statement of the melody.

The AABA scheme appears in the traditional 32-bar musical song in sections of 8 measures each. It occasionally features slight variations in section length, tempo, melody, rhythm, or harmony to provide variety to the song. It may also have an introductory verse to cue the song, as "You Are Love" does in *Show Boat*.

In recent years, however, musical song forms have changed dramatically, both in pop and traditional examples. Following are examples of some of the significant variations on the 32-bar scheme:

"Sunny Side of the Street"	32
"Yesterday" (The Beatles)	29
"If Ever I Would Leave You" (*Camelot*)	52
"If I Loved You" (*Carousel*)	36
"Greensleeves"	16

To prepare for musical performance, it is useful to obtain basic musical theory training and perhaps ear training. Such an introduction to musical theory will be a foundation upon which your musical director may build. An introductory course in sight reading would also further your development in musical theatre performance.

THE VOICE

One of the primary tools of interpretation is an expressive voice, which provides clues to character. To succeed in musical performance it is imperative to "tune" your voice in regular practice sessions that include voice production.

The rehearsal periods devoted to voice training should emphasize the following aspects, concentrating on the best possible diction and an individual interpretation that communicates the subtleties of character, mood, and emotion.

1. *Breathing*. Diaphragmatic breathing is essential if you are to appear relaxed and free of vocal tension. It provides the lung expansion necessary to sustain a performance, and also provides rhythmic air pressure with the least strain or exertion.

2. *Articulation*. Good articulation, or distinctness of speech sounds, is essential. Good articulation helps to form the sounds, syllables, and words that vocalize thoughts, emotions, and attitudes.

3. *Pronunciation*. Correct pronunciation, free of regional influences or colloquialisms, is essential if you are to assume a variety of roles. It is also essential to crisp and clear dialogue or song requiring rapid speech.

4. *Rate*. Variety in rate is essential to suggest character mood, tempo, emphasis, or thought. A desirable rate is one that is energetic, stimulating, and appropriate to both the context of the dialogue or song and the content of the scene.

5. *Volume*. A basic principle of volume in musical performance is a force and emphasis that will permit the voice to be heard and understood by the audience. Variety in volume also permits ideas and emotions to be highlighted.

6. *Quality*. Quality, or vocal timbre, is your "vocal fingerprint" and should be pleasant to hear and yet flexible enough to convey a variety of moods and attitudes. Expressive quality also assists in subtly reinforcing the interpretation with shades and tones of meaning in dialogue or song.

7. *Projection*. Proper projection, or the ability to direct the voice to specific areas of the auditorium, is essential to a vibrant voice capable of being heard and understood by every member of the audience. Projection involves controlled use of the entire speech mechanism and is dependent upon good exhalation, phonation, resonation, and articulation to achieve its meaningful effects.

8. *Animation*. The enthusiasm and energy that characterize the voice are essential to create

The role of the body in interpretation of the character is generally determined by the musical character's age, social position, mood, attitude, or objective in a given scene. In *CAROUSEL*, for example, each character's visual portrait suggests what the character is thinking and anticipating (from the Berea Summer Theatre (Ohio) production. Directed by Neal Poole. Designed by Douglas Hall.)

the vocal tapestry that reveals nuances of thought and meaning. Animation in the voice also commands audience attention.

THE BODY

Another primary tool in interpretation of character is a flexible body. The role of the body involves movement patterns, posture, and physical reactions that reflect the character's motivation and inner thought. To a great extent, use of the body depends upon the choreographer's design for the production,

but there are also creative possibilities in movement inherent in the actions of the character in nonsinging or nondancing scenes.

The role of the body is generally determined by the character's age, social position, mood, or objective in a given scene. The visual portrait should be consistent with what the script/book suggests about the character. Any movement or physical reactions should be fluid and yet clearly indicative of what the character is thinking or anticipating.

The body alone is sometimes sufficient to suggest the character's initial mood or attitude. It not only indicates the mental state of the character but also helps the audience to visualize the context in which later dialogue or song may be delivered. In addition, the use of the body creates a dramatic sense of externalizing the character's motivation and relationship to other characters, as well as to the storyline.

Because the musical is such an individual, creative art form, no attempt is made to formulate a set of rules for the final presentation, other than to say that your performance should be polished.

Final choices of movement, gesture, business, interpretation, and characterization should be determined through observation, detailed analysis of the script/book, and ample rehearsal.

The spirit of vitality and responsibility should help to eliminate some of the initial anxiety associated with musical performance, but there is never a substitute for the motto "Be prepared." Concentration is the most obvious means of preparation, but perhaps these further suggestions will encourage you to give a truly inspired peformance:

The role of the body in suggesting a musical character involves movement patterns, posture, and physical reactions that reflect the character's motivation and inner thought. In *The Roar of the Greasepaint, the Smell of the Crowd*, for example, the chorus captures the essential ingredients of social position and attitude to suggest their inner thoughts. (From the production of the University of Florida. Directed by Joe Conger; set design by Ann Schreck; costume design by Steve Bornstein; choreography by Eric Nielsen. Photography by Albert Wehlburg.)

- Thoroughly analyze the musical as to the sequence of action and songs and the relationship of your character to others in individual scenes.
- Base your performance upon the suggestions found in the dialogue, songs, and stage directions. Supplement this approach to characterization with observation, research, and rehearsal to give added dimension and meaning to your performance.
- Play the role with sufficient variety in voice and body to distinguish the character in the dialogue and action of each scene.
- Present a consistent, energetic portrait of the character that is compatible with what the script/book specifies.
- Make creative use of your own imagination in the creation of the character, and avoid stereotypical approaches.
- Eliminate personal mannerisms and concentrate on a character portrait that is vibrant and honest.

OTHER CONSIDERATIONS

To understand the role of the musical in its performance and production potential, it is necessary to determine its genre, or type. Although easy classifications are not always possible, the following chart should help to clarify the types of musicals despite inevitable duplications, similarities, and overlapping.

Type	Characteristics
Musical revue	Series of separate songs, dances, and skits; usually comic or satiric; loosely based on a theme or unified point of view; presentational style. Examples: *Oh, Calcutta!, Mayor*, and *Forbidden Broadway*.
Musical comedy	Comic book with integrated songs and dances; musical subplots; series of loosely connected scenes or episodes; sequential dialogue; initial character development. Examples: *Forty-Second Street, Annie Get Your Gun*, and *How to Succeed in Business Without Really Trying*.
Musical drama	Serious topic; emphasis upon song and dance to convey meaning; score and plot reinforcing book; complex character development; element of comedy reduced; dramatic rather than comic moments. Examples: *Cats, Fiddler on the Roof*, and *West Side Story*.
Musical opera	Sophisticated music from primarily popular sources; less dance than traditional musical; three-dimensional characterization; literary book or script; frequently based on other literary sources. Examples: *Porgy and Bess* and *Jesus Christ, Superstar*.
Operetta	Short, amusing musical play; satire or parody of another source or event; lyrical in tone; emphasizes fantasy or dream-like scenes or episodes. Examples: *The King and I, Brigadoon*, and *Carousel*.

As you begin to explore your own role in the musical theatre, pay special attention to the skills you need to develop to be a successful and accomplished performer. In particular, consider your age, type, area of specialty, vocal technique, acting ability, range, movement skills, and stage experience. It is useful to secure a good voice teacher who can develop your range and flexibility. It is further beneficial to build a routine of exercises and activities to secure acting and movement teachers who have extensive experience in performance techniques, auditions, and dance exercises.

BASIC EXERCISES

The beginning musical theatre performer may discover in the rehearsal period some creative exercises that are appropriate for his or her own style of performance. The following exercises are presented as exploratory experiences to help you reach the techniques of voice and movement that are essential to a stimulating musical performance. Each exercise is framed as a working blueprint to stimulate awareness of the principles of musical theatre performance; to promote development of believable characterization; and to provide the ingredients of vocal and physical performance.

PHON-A-THON

The pitch of the voice can be accurately measured by the rate of vibration of the vocal bands. The subsequent sound may vary according to the position and the degree of tenseness or relaxation of the vocal folds. The quality of the voice may also be influenced by the capacity of the vocal bands to respond to vibrations in a frequency best suited to utilize the vocal resonators, the air chambers in the head and throat that help to amplify and enrich sound.

In cultivating a relaxed throat and neck to achieve greater flexibility and range in pitch and

tone, pay attention to your breathing in this phonation exercise. When you inhale, purse your lips and make a whistling sound with the inflowing air. When you exhale, do so with an *ah* sound. Your mouth should be open, without muscle tension in either the face or the throat. The sound produced should resemble that which people make when leaning over a cradle to ''coo'' at an infant.

Repeat each exercise three times in sequence before moving on to the next series.

1. On a single breath, begin to count aloud until you feel tension or strain in your vocal cords. Work until you can increase original count by 25%. For example, if your original count is 40, work easily until you can expand the count to at least 50. Remember, *no tension!*

   Count at a steady and regular pace until your capacity to sustain breath reaches a comfortable count, generally 60 on a single breath. It helps to count to a metronome set at Allegro, which is 138 beats per minute.

   Now, standing upright with your arms relaxed at your sides, begin to yawn. Repeat the yawn several times, freeing the vocal mechanism from tension. Then follow the sequence below to activate the phonation process.

   a. ''Catch'' a yawn at its most open point by pinching your nose shut and phonating an *ah* with a pitch much lower than your normal one. Repeat five times.
   b. Begin to control the cycle. On the next *yawn-ah* series, prolong the sound to the count of 10. Repeat the sequence, adding one more count until you reach 15. Repeat the 15 count of *ah* another five times.
   c. Omit the yawn and inhale with the whistling sound to the count of 15, making sure that you also exhale with an *ah* to the same count.

d. When you are pleased with the *ah* sound, gradually increase your sound count to 20.

At no time should you feel any vibration in the nasal cavities. If you do feel nasal vibration or a "twang" sound, you are forcing part of the *ah* sound through your nose. Repeat this part of the exercise 10 times, or until the vibrations have ceased.

2. Standing upright, rest your fingers lightly on the tip of your nostrils. Repeat the following sequences as you concentrate on disciplined use of inhalation to produce good phonation.

a. On a single breath, repeat the vowel sounds of the following words 10 times. Pause only between the sounding of the words. Do not inhale until the sound has been produced the tenth time.

*ea*t	p*ur*se	cl*o*se
c*a*n	sl*aw*	n*oo*n
l*aw*	p*u*p	r*o*t

For example, the word *eat* begins the exercise with a voicing of the *ea* sound. That is followed by a brief pause, another sounding of the *ea*, then another brief pause. Continue this pattern until you have sounded *ea* 10 times and are ready to inhale.

b. Repeat the vowel sounds of the following words in the manner described above. Take care not to inhale until the completion of the sequence.

h*a*t	s*oa*p	s*oo*n
r*o*t	l*aw*	p*u*p
d*ie*	h*i*s	n*o*se
c*a*n	f*a*t	k*i*ck
use	f*o*g	pl*ea*

c. Repeat the exercise until you can voice each vowel 15 times on a single breath. Remember, however, that there should be no vibration sound in your nostrils.

POETRY IN MOTION

The role of the body in conveying character is of primary importance in creating a relaxed, natural portrait of self-confidence and poise. In this exercise, your goal is to voice the following lines from William Wordworth's "Evening on Calais Beach," using only gestures and movement to suggest the meaning. (Later, substitute the lyrics of your musical song and communicate the meaning using only gestures while you sing the words).

First, analyze the poem to determine the probable setting and mood, then decide on an appropriate age for the character described. Next, perform the poem silently with subtle gestures and movements to convey the action described by the poet. Be sure that your "performance" builds to a climax. Gestures and movements should be fluid and flexible, executed with vigor and strength. Use only those absolutely necessary to convey the meaning.

Repeat this silent performance three times, refining your gestures and movements while you "*suit the action to the word*," as Hamlet urges in his famous advice to the players. You may then wish to videotape another performance for comparison with later performances.

"It is a beauteous evening, calm and free,
The holy time is quiet as a nun
Breathless with adoration; the broad sun
Is sinking down in its tranquility;
The gentleness of heaven broods o'er the sea:
Listen! the mighty being is awake,
And doth with his eternal motion make
A sound like thunder—everlastingly.
Dear child! dear girl! that walkest
with me here,
If thou appear untouched by solemn thought,
Thy nature is not therefore less divine:
Thou liest in Abraham's bosom all the year;
And worship'st at the temple's inner shrine,
God being with thee when we know it not."

When you feel that you understand the role of the voice in giving depth and dimension to the character your gestures and movement created, repeat the exercise. This time, however, ''sing'' the passage in a relaxed, appropriate tone of voice and in a key that suggests each of the following situations borrowed from typical musical plots.

- A young lover mourning the loss of a sweetheart. (*West Side Story*)
- A young woman saddened by loneliness. (*Song of Bernadette*)
- A cunning man plotting his revenge. (*Fiorello!*)
- A villain stalking the hero. (*Oklahoma!*)
  A young girl singing a song of sorrow. (*A Little Night Music*)
- An older character recalling her youth and joy. (*Gypsy*)

Conclude the exercise by incorporating the gestures and movements developed earlier as you perform the passage again. Are your gestures and movements compatible with your voice? Are they natural and relaxed in comparison with your vocal tone? Are they subtle enough to reinforce your conversational vocal tone? What adjustments must you make to your performance?

When you are confident that your voice and movement are working together to intepret *and* to sing the poem, tape record the vocal part of the exercise as an example of the vocal tone needed to communicate effectively in performance. Use it as a model for subsequent character portraits and continue to work on meaningful gestures and movement to reinforce the lyrics of songs.

FREEING THE NATURAL VOICE

Remember that proper breathing frees the natural voice for expressive tone and dimension. When a constant stream of air is breathed into the lungs, the diaphragm contracts and enlarges the chest cavity to sustain a rich, full-throated sound. As the air is released from the lungs, the diaphragm expands to its original position and reduces the size of the chest cavity, thus completing the sound-making process.

In the exercise that follows, concentrate on the basic techniques of proper breathing and breath control to enhance your natural voice and to develop the capacity to sustain vibrant and vital sound. Begin the exercise by lying flat on your back and breathing normally. Notice how the midsection of your body rises and falls as you inhale and exhale. Now place a heavy book on your stomach and continue to breathe deeply. Is there more or less movement of the midsection now? (Perhaps the book is too heavy?)

Continue this part of the exercise until you can easily and freely raise and lower the book without straining your abdomen. Next, remove the book and place your hands on your stomach as you breathe deeply *without raising your shoulders*. Do you feel any tension or strain now? Do you feel the muscles of the stomach expanding both in the midsection and at the sides? Continue this part of the exercise for successive counts of 10, 20, 30, 40, and 50.

When you are comfortable with your breathing and there is less tension in your midsection, repeat each of the following passages using only one breath. Do not rush your pronunciation of the words; try to sustain your sound until the last word of each phrase.

''There'll always be an England
  While there's a busy street,
Whenever there's a turning wheel,
  A million marching feet.''

''Soldiers are dreamers; when the guns begin
They think of firelit homes, clean beds,
  and wives.''

''And when the war is done and
  youth stone dead
I'd toddle safely home and die—
  in bed.''

''There is not a woman in the world the possession of whom is as precious as that of the truths which she reveals to us by causing us to suffer.

We are healed of a suffering only by experiencing it to the full.''

Now stand before a full-length mirror and observe your breathing. If your chest or your shoulders rise when you breathe, it should suggest that you are not making proper use of the diaphragm and that you need to correct your posture as well.

Remain at the mirror and begin the second part of the exercise by inhaling and exhaling normally. Then take a deep breath and exhale slowly, sustaining the sound ''ah'' for a count of 15. Relax, then take a deeper breath and exhale slowly, sustaining the ''ah'' sound for a count of 20. Relax, and repeat, sustaining the ''ah'' sound as long as possible on a single breath. Do not try to aid the exhalation process by whispering or by rushing the sound.

When you are able to sustain the exhalation for a count of at least 25, repeat the following passage from Robert Benchley's *Do You Make These Mistakes?* by freeing your natural voice. Try to sustain your breath control by pausing only when necessary for clarity of meaning, by keeping the exhalation process to at least a count of 25, and by taking deep inhalations.

> ''A great many people use faulty English without knowing it. Ain't you? How many times, for instance, have you wanted to use the word 'eleemosynary' and haven't been able to do so without laughing? So you have used 'whom' instead, thinking that it means the same thing. Well, it don't—doesn't! You may think that these little slips, and others like them, do not matter in ordinary conversation. 'I make myself understood, don't I?' you may say. Ah, but do you?
>
> ''A man in Colorado was hanged for murder because in a written statement he said, 'I did it,' instead of 'I didn't do it.' Napoleon failed to take Moscow until it was a mass of ruins because he said: 'Take your time, Joe!' instead of 'Hurry up, Joe!' to the man who had charge of the army. Just the difference of three little words!

> ''But is no reason why you should be at sea. All that is needed is a few hours' practice every day, being careful not to bend the knees. Just keep saying to yourself, over and over again, 'I *shall* speak good English!' Before long, you will find yourself saying, 'I *will* speak good English!' or possibly just, 'The hell with it!' ''

CHARACTER BUILDING BLOCKS

One of the primary elements of good musical theatre characterization is the ability to use personal observation to build a believable portrait, one that both ''speaks'' and ''sings'' expressively. You need to observe people by listening to what they say and by noticing how they express themselves. Observe their tone of voice and see if it is related to their occupation, personality, or status. Listen to their pattern of inflection, rate of speaking, and pitch of voice to discover vocal patterns that might be of value in developing an interesting character portrait.

You can learn a great deal about observation and its role in building characterization from visiting places where people congregate in large numbers: railway stations, supermarkets, fairgrounds, malls, sporting events, or even crowded streets in large cities. Take a tape recorder with you to capture your impressions for later review. Talk with people, listen to them, and try to learn more about them. Your interest needs to be genuine inquiry, not idle curiosity. Gather as much information as you can, including age, height, weight, occupation, interests, and attitudes.

Gather information from at least ten persons such as a teacher, a factory worker, an athlete, a waiter, a lawyer, a custodian, a salesperson, a government official, an entertainer, and a politician. Make a checklist of the general characteristics associated with each occupation. Pay particular attention to vocal and physical characteristics that might later be incorporated into creative characterizations like the actors in *A Chorus Line*, the grande dame in *A*

Little Night Music, the politicians in *Fiorello!,* or the gang leaders in *West Side Story.*

Make sure your checklist includes those elements of characterization that help to define personality:

1. Vocal presence
2. Physical presence
3. Age
4. Attitude
5. Mood
6. Clothes

All of these elements are closely interrelated, each affecting the others to some degree. Try to combine the elements in the following "interview" sessions.

Choose one of your observed personalities to role-play. Review the tape recording of his or her vocal presence, then assume the physical presence. Add to your characterization the appropriate age, attitude, or mood that you observed. You may also wish to reinforce your characterization by wearing clothes that capture the spirit and temperament of your observed person.

Next, improvise an interview session as if your observed character were being considered for the positions described. Walk to the interview in the physical presence of your character, speak in the vocal presence of your character, and assume the age, attitude, and mood of your character. Then respond to the following questions posed by the interviewer.

One of the primary performance elements of good musical theatre characterization is the ability to use personal observation to build a believable character portrait. The creative ability to integrate personal observation into performance results in individualized characters that are easily distinguished from other group characters in the production. (From the production of *FLORADORA*, staged by the University of Minnesota Centennial Showboat. Directed and choreographed by Robert Moulton. Scenery and props designed by C. Lance Brockman. Costume design by Christine Vesper. Lighting design by Jean Montgomery.)

I. Interview for a Job
   a) Where have you worked before?
   b) Do you have any references?
   c) What are your skills?
   d) What are your goals?
   e) Can you type?

II. Interview for a Replacement Position
   a) How did you learn of the job?
   b) Are you available immediately?
   c) Can you work late evenings?
   d) Do you have transportation?
   e) Do you have a police record?

When you have completed both interview sessions, tape record your responses as you and your character interview a second time. Then compare that recording with the initial one made of the observed personality. Were you able to capture the vocal presence of your initial observation? What about similarities in attitude and mood? What about similarities in physical presence and age?

Complete the exercise by role-playing each of your other observed and tape-recorded personalities in the two interviews. Pay particular attention to recreating the vocal and physical presence and incorporate appropriate changes in attitude and mood from your first tape recording of the personality. When you have completed this exercise, you should have discovered a formula for using observation, tape recording, and role-playing to building imaginative characterizations for musical theatre performance.

Part II

ACTING IN
MUSICAL THEATRE

ACTING IN MUSICAL THEATRE

There is no such person as the "beginning actor." We have all been "acting" or "impersonating" more or less instinctively from early childhood. Our youthful games of "pretend" and "make believe" have given us the basic ingredients to *assume* roles in any given musical script. Our stories, deceptions, and disguises have given us the ingredients to *convince* an audience that what "might have been" is, indeed, "what was." And our repeated experiences, observations, and individual patterns of behavior have given us the ingredients to *sustain* believable thoughts and actions.

Any serious study of acting, however, suggests that there must be more involved in this creative art form; that it must involve degrees of skill and varying methods of approach or performance blueprints. Indeed, the successful musical performance *is* carefully orchestrated and has its greatest impact when the performer possesses a certain degree of skill, a unique method of character creation, and a believable performance blueprint that is at once competent and creative.

But musical scripts vary and different styles of playing demand a variety of approaches. You should not become inhibited by relying on only *one* approach to discovering your individual technique. Nor should you limit the possibilities for creative invention that come with careful preparation and rehearsal. Your primary responsibility is to communicate the character and the song of the musical to an audience with as much truthfulness and honesty as possible.

PREREQUISITES
FOR PERFORMANCE

Before proceeding to a performance blueprint, it is necessary to point out some of the prerequisites that the musical performer should be aware of as he or she approaches the creation and development of a character.

First, the performer should be *knowledgeable.* That implies an understanding of basic theatrical and musical techniques and conventions. Being knowledgeable also suggests familiarity with the principles of the musical style of performance and possession of the "mimetic instinct," or the ability to imitate other human beings.

Second, the performer should be *disciplined.* That implies not only a controlled and orderly system of preparation and rehearsal, but also an efficiency of acting and singing technique that suggests to an audience that the performance is spontaneous and true-to-life, not contrived or artificial. Being disciplined also suggests that the performer has planned the performance in detail, not relied solely upon spontaneous impulse or improvisation and has created the role within a framework of detailed analysis and evaluation of the musical book.

Third, the performer should be *innovative.* That implies giving the performance added dimension by original invention and interpretation. This essential ingredient of creativity also suggests that the performer has achieved a degree of uninhibited abandon necessary to assume the role of the character he or she is portraying. In addition, being innovative suggests that the performer has an indescribable "life-spirit" that not only stimulates the imagination of the audience but also enriches the character portrait being drawn.

Some other important prerequisites for musical performance include the following:

- The performer should have wide experience from which to draw the character portrait. The wider the range of experience, the more sensitive and complex the portrait is likely to be.

- The performer's own personality should be the initial source from which the character portrait is molded and given life. The primary performance goal is to explore his or her own personality as a key to discovering creative role-playing.
- The performer's skills must include intensive training of *both* the voice and the body as expressive instruments that help to delineate character.
- The performer should be flexible and yet well informed regarding the character, the scenes, the dialogue, and the songs and should study the script for interpretation and movement hints to assist in the creation of a lively interpretation of the character.
- The performer should cultivate a catalog of sensory and emotional responses that might be recalled when needed to suggest the energy, the tempo, the mood, or the attitude of the character in performance.

Like the cub reporter, the musical performer should approach the creation of a role with discipline and careful research that details the *who, what, where, when,* and *why* of both the character and the scene.

Begin the creation of the role by exploring the dimensions of the character in his or her relationship to the complete musical. The exploration should include an analysis of what the character is thinking or feeling in a given scene and his or her motivation and attitude in relation to others in the scene. In addition, it should detail the opportunities for movement or interaction with the audience and search for the bodily actions and gestures that will communicate ideas or emotions in either the dialogue or the songs.

In the evolution of this carefullly planned period of analysis, you may actually begin to assume the role of the character and, in the creative process of vocal and physical adjustment, begin to shape your character portrait. You may even discover that personal traits and complementary behavior may be integrated into the portrait to create a composite of *person/actor* that adds dimension and purpose to your characterization.

A useful way to begin character building is to pay careful attention to the lines your character speaks or sings, for the true character is revealed in both dialogue and songs. Take note also of any changes that take place in the character during the action of the script. You may even find it helpful to make an outline, or ''performance chart,'' of the character's personality traits and thoughts as they are revealed by speeches or songs made *to* or *about* him or her. Give your chart appropriate main headings that provide some dimension and permit you almost to visualize how the character will appear, speak, and sing. Questions you might answer as you prepare your chart include:

- How does the character react to other characters?
- What stage business or detailed action does the character repeat frequently?
- Is the character suffering from any maladjustments?
- How do the character's personal habits and attitudes influence the actions of other characters?
- Where does the character appear to place priorities?
- What adjectives clarify the character's point of view? For example, is the character primarily fearful, playful, shy, friendly, aggressive, envious, cautious, or talkative?
- Which other characters appear to influence your character the most, the least?
- What are the character's primary objectives in each scene?
- What significant changes of attitude are made by the character, and in which scenes do they occur?
- What do the song lyrics reveal about the character's mood and attitude?
- How would you describe the character's mental and emotional state of mind?

As you become better acquainted with your character in rehearsal, you may wish to include observation, informal discussion, and role models in your performance blueprint. Observation, whether planned or casual, provides information gained by direct experience and has the additional benefit of vitality and local color when used in building a character portrait. Alertness to events in everyday life provides the gestures, the attitude, the voice, the walk, the mannerisms that give individuality to characterization. The performer who is sensitive and aware may also discover the creative satisfaction of transferring what has been noted from everyday life into a viable, believable stage portrait.

Informal discussions, whether with friends or strangers, often result in insights that help in developing an initial character portrait. Probably the best known of such informal discussions that assisted a performer in fashioning a character portrait involved silent film star Charlie Chaplin. While walking in San Francisco, Chaplin met a hobo and invited him to lunch. The hobo related the sad story of his life: long jaunts through the countryside, frightening rides on freighters and trains, and the personal misfortunes that often accompany the out-

Musical characterization may include observation, informal discussion, and role models incorporated into the performance blueprint. In *ANNIE*, for example, performance role models may include the cartoon strip upon which the characterizations are based. (From the production of the Berea Summer Theatre (Ohio). Directed by Joseph J. Garry, Jr. Set design by Douglas Hall. Choreography by Suzanne Strew.)

cast. From these descriptions and revelations, Chaplin created his immortal "little tramp."

As valuable as all of these preliminary resources may be, however, the musical performer's most important resource for character creation remains imagination and creativity. There will be characters for which the most careful analysis and observation cannot provide the clue necessary to sketch a meaningful portrait; you must then rely upon imagination and creativity to provide the spark that illuminates the character and the scene.

CHARACTER INTERPRETATION

One of the most challenging responsibilities for the musical performer is to interpret the character objectively as a means of shedding light on the meaning of the musical. Character interpretation implies careful analysis of what the author/lyricist has suggested about the character. The critical skills of research and the creative skills of impersonation should combine to communicate the meaning of both the character's dialogue and the subsequent action.

It is also important in character interpretation to learn the art of "acting a song." A traditional theatre scene is considerably longer than a musical theatre song, and that timing is the key to interpretation. You must learn to "speak" in the tempo of the song and to voice "lines" on pitch. Remember, also, that most musicals have a poetic lyric, and that you must "act" several beats in advance of what you are speaking or singing.

In approaching a song in performance, it is helpful to know the motivation and dramatic intent of the song, to whom it is being sung, where the action of the song *and* the scene is taking place, and what subtext is revealed by the song. It is useful to copy the song lyrics in a looseleaf notebook, and to approach rehearsal of the song just as you might work on a traditional theatre scene. Also consider the role that facial expressions, gestures, movement, emotional responses, or physical reactions might play in giving dimension and scope to your interpretation.

Character interpretation is a way to fill the empty space in musicals when performers stand stage center to sing directly to the audience. Imagine the song as a scene between you and another, invisible acting partner. Direct your attention toward the audience, move with poise and grace, and exhibit the self-confidence and vitality that help to display your vocal and physical talents.

ADDITIONAL PERFORMANCE PERSPECTIVES

In musical theatre there must always be "vocal orchestration" that allows the performer to interpret the dialogue of the book and to voice the dynamic sounds of the libretto. By polishing your vocal instrument, it is possible to highlight meaning, focus attention, and direct listener interest. For these reasons it is important to pay careful attention to the vocal attributes responsible for meaningful interpretation of dialogue or libretto.

The speech and vocalization process is so intricate that for our purposes it must be confined to those essentials that are necessary for the musical theatre performer to become "voice-conscious" rather than "voice-confused."

In describing the elements involved in the vocal production of sound, it is convenient to divide the process into four areas: *breathing, phonation, resonance,* and *articulation*. In performance, however, these areas function as an integrated unit under the control of the central nervous system. They are treated separately here to isolate areas that have specific problems.

BREATHING

Proper breathing makes good use of the diaphragm, a thin, broad muscle that separates the chest cavity (or *thorax*) from the abdominal cavity. When air is breathed into the lungs (*inhalation*), the diaphragm contracts and enlarges the chest cavity sufficiently to sustain sound. When air is subsequently released from the lungs (*exhalation*), the diaphragm expands to its original position and re-

In approaching the song in performance, it would be helpful to know what the motivation and dramatic intent of the song is in a given scene; to whom the song is being sung; where the action of the song and the scene is taking place; and what subtext is revealed by the song. In *The Roar of the Greasepaint, the Smell of the Crowd*, for example, the performers use facial expressions, gestures, and movement to suggest the emotional content of the song being sung. (From the production of the University of Florida. Directed by Joe Conger; set design by Ann Schreck; costume design by Steve Bornstein; choreography by Eric Nielsen. Photography by Albert Wehlburg.)

duces the size of the chest cavity, thus completing the sound-making process.

Diaphragmatic breathing provides the greatest lung expansion, is least likely to cause tension in the vocal muscles, and provides the necessary rhythmic air pressure with the least strain or exertion. In approaching the principle of diaphragmatic breathing, remember that frequent inhalations are more desirable than occasional deep inhalations, and that in exhalation it should be possible to start or stop the process with ease. Remember also that the diaphragm is active only during inhalation; during exhalation it does little more than relax and encourage quiet breathing.

A good test of the stream of air needed for efficient sound production is as follows. Lie flat on your back and relax completely. Place your hand just above the waistline and begin to breathe slowly and deeply. As you breathe, pay particular attention to the expansion and contraction of the diaphragm muscle and notice how the abdominal wall appears to move in and out as the breathing is consciously directed and controlled.

After several minutes, or long enough to realize how proper diaphragmatic breathing feels, stand up and repeat the exercise. Keep your hand at the waist to detect any change in the center of breathing, and recite a favorite slogan or nonsense phrase. If breathing appears to be centered in the upper chest and the abdominal wall is not actively in motion, practice slower and deeper breathing. Encourage the diaphragm to expand and contract with a comfortable rhythm, and concentrate on preventing the upper chest from rising and falling. Repeat this exercise for several short periods during the day, and the results should be improved voice production and control.

PHONATION

Phonation is vibration of the vocal folds to produce the tone of the voice. By locating the *larynx*, or "voice box," you will notice that two muscles stretch across it from front to back. In ordinary breathing, these small bands of muscle remain in a relaxed position so that air may pass through them without causing vibration. In speaking or singing, however, the two bands tighten and the air from the lungs must be forced through them. When this air strikes the vocal bands it sets them vibrating, and the result is sound waves that amplify and give variation to the pitch of the voice.

The fundamental pitch of the voice, therefore, may be accurately measured by the rate of vibration of the vocal bands, and the sound of the voice varies according to the position and the degree of tenseness or relaxation of the vocal folds. The quality of the voice is also influenced by the capacity of the vocal bands to respond to vibrations in a frequency best suited to utilize vocal resonators, the air chambers in the head and throat that help to amplify and enrich sound.

The performer can make little adjustment in the role that the larynx plays in vocal production because the muscles that stimulate the vocal bands to move closer together or farther apart are not subject to conscious control. They are controlled only as a group, and then only indirectly as the throat is open and free for the emission of sound. Hence, any desired change in pitch should be approached more as exercises in ear training and unconscious positioning of the bands than as vocal cord training.

There are, however, certain principles involved in relaxing the throat and the neck to achieve greater flexibility in pitch and tone quality. Knowing that the sound of the voice will vary according to the position and the degree of tenseness or relaxation in the vocal cords, practice the following exercise:

Slowly drop your head forward and allow the lower jaw to sag. Yawn several times as the head gently sways from left to right, and then from right to left. Allow the head to return to its normal full-front position, and slowly sound each of the vowels, *a, e, i, o,* and *u.* Breathe quietly, using a soft tone. Repeat the vowel sounds, prolonging each for three or four seconds. Repeat the vowel sounds again, using a slightly louder tone. Repeat the vowel sounds again, using a slightly softer tone. Now repeat the vowel sounds using a lower pitch, then a lower pitch, and then a still lower pitch until you are producing the lowest pitch possible without strain or tension. Repeat the vowel sounds using a higher pitch, then a higher pitch, and then a still higher pitch until you are producing the highest pitch possible without undue strain or tension.

Relax! You are well on your way to freeing the voice and achieving the pitch variety and tone quality that are necessary for flexibility in vocal performance. You may wish to complete the exploration of phonation by using what you have learned about your individual pitch range and vocal quality to read aloud, with as much variety as possible, the following excerpt from William Shakespeare's narrative poem, *"Venus and Adonis."*

> For pity now she can no more detain him;
> The poor fool prays her that he may depart:
> She is resolved no longer to restrain him,
> Bids him farewell, and look well to her heart.
> > The which, by Cupid's bow
> > > she doth protest,
> > He carries thence incaged in his breast.

> 'Sweet boy,' she says,
> > 'this night I'll waste in sorrow,
> For my sick heart commands
> > mine eyes to watch.
> Tell me, Love's master,
> > shall we meet to-morrow?
> Say, shall we? shall we?
> > wilt though make the match?'
> > > He tells her no; to-morrow he intends
> > > To hunt the boar with certain of his
> > > friends.

RESONANCE

Resonance refers to the amplification and enrichment of sound as it passes along the vocal folds. The three cavities most responsible for resonance are the throat (*pharynx*), the mouth, and the nose.

Sound waves are amplified and reinforced by being reflected by these cavities in the fashion of a megaphone or pipes in an organ. Their flexibility in both shape and size is responsible for the variation of voice necessary for expressive dialogue or singing. At the same time, sounds may also be modified by consciously changing the shape and the size of the throat and the mouth, or by allowing or preventing the escape of air through the nasal cavities. It is in this way that various consonant and vowel sounds are formed.

The most important principle to note in resonation is that the flexibility needed for vocal variety usually occurs spontaneously as mood, attitude, and expression change. Practical application of resonation, however, can produce all of the generally recognized voice qualities.

For example, there is the *guttural*, or throaty, quality; the high-pitched, *falsetto*, quality; the breathy, or *aspirate*, quality; the low-pitched, *pectoral,* quality; the "perpetual cold," or *nasal*, quality; and the *normal* quality. It should be pointed out, however, that the normal quality is not the same for all performers. It is simply the accepted standard of performance and represents a balanced use of all three resonating cavities. The normal quality of the voice is continuously pleasant, mellow, and conversational with sufficient vocal variation to suggest changing mood and attitude.

Beginning musical theatre performers are sometimes frustrated with their dominant vocal quality (*tenor, baritone,* or *bass*) because they have imagined that it is possible to acquire a "new," perhaps more dramatic, voice. Not so! Just as no two human beings are totally alike, so also no two voices are ever exactly alike, and imitation of a "desirable" vocal quality in another performer is sure to result in affectation and artifice.

Remember that the term "vocal quality" describes only the general characteristics that distinguish one voice from another when both voices are similar in rate, pitch, and volume. A bass voice or a tenor voice may be equally effective if it is sufficiently animated to allow resonation to provide the spontaneous flexibility needed for expressiveness and effective delivery of dialogue or song.

A good exercise to familiarize yourself with the resonance cavities is humming or chanting. Begin by relaxing the muscles of the neck and throat, much as in the previous exercise for phonation. Close the lips lightly, leaving the jaws relaxed and open. Sound the letter *n* until you feel the vibration in the nasal cavities. Prolong the sound for as long as possible on a single breath. Now open the mouth and add vowels to the *n*, producing the sounds for *na, ne, ni, no,* and *nu*. Next, produce a series of short, chantlike sounds starting with a prolonged *n-n-n-n,* and follow in sequence with *ah-ah-ah-ah-ah; oo-oo-oo-oo-oo; ing, ing, ing, ing, ing;* and *ee-ee-ee-ee-ee.*

Note the vibrations produced by the sounds and their placement in the cavity responsible for the sounds. This is the beginning of an exploration of the many tones of resonance possible for an attractive and pleasing vocal quality. Complete an exercise by reading aloud the following selection from Alfred Lord Tennyson's "The Lotos-Eaters," paying particular attention to the individual words that should be voiced by the important resonance cavities. Maintain good breath control during this exercise, and open the mouth as freely as possible to encourage efficient resonation. Continue to repeat the exercise—finally singing the selection—until you are able to produce the richness of tone and the distinctive vowel quality that are part of the proper resonation.

> There is sweet music here that softer falls
> Than petals from blown roses on the grass,
> Or night-dews on still waters between walls
> Of shadowy granite, in a gleaming pass;
> Music that gentlier on the spirit lies,
> Than tir'd eyelids upon tir'd eyes;
> Music that brings sweet sleep down from
>   the blissful skies.
> Here are cool mosses deep,
> And thro' the moss the ivies creep,
> And in the stream the long-leaved
>   flowers weep,
> And from the craggy ledge
>   the poppy hangs in sleep.

ARTICULATION

After the vibration of the air in the vocal bands of the larynx has been resonated in the cavities of the head and the throat, there remains but the *articulation* of speech sounds to produce recognizable consonants and vowels. The role of articulation, which may be defined as the distinctness with which speech sounds are formed, is reserved specifically for the *lips, tongue, teeth, hard palate, soft palate* (velum), and *jaw.* These "articulators" help to form sounds, syllables, and words.

Slovenly articulation is among the most common faults of the beginning performer, and among the primary causes are "lazy lips" and stage fright. For example, when a performer is nervous or overly cautious there is a tendency to tighten the facial muscles, tense the jaws and lips, and close the mouth rather tightly. The result is a "ventriloquist" approach to speaking or singing.

Five principal types of articulation problems inhibit the ability to pronounce words distinctly. The performer may *omit* sounds, *substitute* one sound for another, *reverse* a sound, *add* a sound, or *misplace stress* of a sound. Omission is failure to utter the correct sound; substitution is replacing a correct sound with an incorrect one; reversal is transposing the position of a sound; addition is incorporating extra vowels or consonants; and misplaced stress is incorrect accenting of a word.

Remember that skill in articulation requires knowledge of the accepted pronunciation of all the words you speak or sing. Pronunciation errors distract listeners and give a negative impression. The lesson is obvious: Correct pronunciation suggests an ability to engage in intelligible conversation or song that reflects a communicative approach to the listener.

VOCAL VARIABLES

When the principles of the speech process and the vocal mechanism have been carefully explored, you should turn your attention to the vocal variables that may be employed to give the voice flexibility and variety. *Vocal variety* is the key to effective performance. The first step in achieving it is to recognize the auditory characteristics of a vigorous and vital voice, and then to outline a program of self-evaluation to correct present weaknesses and promote future strengths.

Remember, however, that merely acquainting yourself with the vocal variables will not insure the development of dynamic performance skills. You must practice—and practice frequently—so that your technique appears subtle and distinctly individual. Practice the exercises at the end of this chapter so that your voice is capable of sufficient variety to engage the listener's interest and comprehension.

RATE

Rate refers to the speed with which words are spoken. Although you should have no problem with rate in singing, the speaking rate varies a great deal and is dependent upon use of pauses, verbal facility, and even subject material. In general, a desirable rate of speaking is one that is energetic, stimulating, and appropriate to the content of the speech or the scene. For example, narrative material or descriptive, sequential events that culminate in a sudden climax may be spoken at a faster rate; whereas technical information, exposition, or statistical data usually requires a slower rate to allow the listener time to digest the material.

Some of the most common faults in rate are too many or too few pauses, interjections such as "uh," "er," or "ah" sprinkled throughout the speech, lack of variation in tempo, too many or two few words per minute, an artificial pattern of emphasis that fails to highlight the ideas or the mood being expressed, characteristic reserve and lack of animation in the rhythm of delivery, mechanical intersentence and interphrasal pauses, and stumbling or hesitation.

PITCH

Pitch refers to the general location of the voice high or low on the musical scale. Although location is determined primarily by the physiological structure of the vocal mechanism, there are several recognized ways to vary pitch and achieve greater range and flexibility. The voice may *slide* as you gradually change pitch within a syllable or a word; or the voice may *step* as you abruptly change, or "break," pitch from one syllable or word to another for emphasis.

Another method of achieving pitch variety is to discover your *optimum pitch range*, or the tonal level at which your voice is most easily produced. The optimum range includes all the levels, both high and low, at which the voice can be sounded without strain. Discovering and using the optimum pitch range effectively permits you to move easily up and down the vocal scale for emphasis and dramatic effect.

Your optimum pitch level is relatively easy to discover. You might wish to compare your present vocal tones with the tones of a well-tuned piano. Begin by singing from your lowest possible pitch to your highest possible pitch, using the standard *do-re-mi* musical scale. Match each of your tones with the corresponding tone of the piano. As you sing, note the lowest and the highest possible notes that you can produce without vocal strain or tension.

Your optimum pitch level is approximately two-thirds of the way down the scale from the highest note produced without strain, which should allow you to vary your pitch within a range of at least two octaves. If this newly discovered pitch range is not the one you use most often in normal conversation, consider the exercises at the end of the chapter to find ways of raising and lowering your pitch so that it is expressive and yet apppropriate to your acting and singing situations.

Although development of significant pitch variety depends largely upon natural gifts and professional training, frequent practice and practical experience are the basic tools for promoting greater tonal flexibility.

- Learn to hear your voice as the listener hears it. The first step in learning one's voice is to tape record it and develop an awareness of its range.
- Discover the pitch range best suited to your natural voice, and practice it in conversation.
- Relax the vocal mechanism *before* speaking or singing. The degree of tension in the vocal cords determines your initial pitch; the greater the tension, the higher the pitch.
- Avoid monotony in pitch: *monopitch*, which is the absence of change in pitch or a consistently similar pitch; and *repetitive pitch*, in which the voice assumes a recurrent and predictable pattern of moving up and down.
- Become aware of pitch in everyday conversation, and actively use the pitch variation learned in the study of the vocal variables to give life and meaning to your vocal expressions.

VOLUME

Volume refers to the loudness or softness of the voice. One of the principles of good volume is to give dynamic range to the level of loudness or softness so that there is adequate force and emphasis to permit the performer to be heard and understood. Achieving better variety in volume usually requires variation in the *amount* of force applied to the voice; as, for example, when you whisper to share a confidence or shout to emphasize a declarative statement. Variety in volume may also be suggested in the *degree* of force exhibited; as, for example, when you abrubtly increase your volume to vocally underscore a series of words or phrases, or when you reduce the loudness to subordinate ideas or to stress relationships that have personal meaning.

The ability to increase or decrease volume for emphasis and vocal variety is dependent upon the proper use of the breathing mechanism, vocal cords, and resonators. You should therefore review the mechanics of the breathing process before attempting conscious variety in volume and make use of the exhaled breath that vibrates the vocal cords and amplifies the sound. In addition, while learning to control the amount of force, it is also beneficial to observe what happens to the pitch and the quality of the voice as volume is increased and decreased.

A natural tendency for beginning performers is to raise the pitch whenever they attempt to increase the volume. That only increases muscle tension throughout the speaking mechanism and may result in throaty or hoarse speech. On the other hand, the relaxation produced by arbitrarily lowering pitch to suggest softness may result instead in a breathy quality of speech. The best approach to achieving variety is to maintain an adequate supply of air, learn to breathe deeply, and control exhalation. A good test to evaluate your present technique of breathing and pitch level is to repeat a phrase like, ''*Now* is the *time* for all *good* men to come to the *aid* of their *country*.''

Emphasize each of the italicized words with varying degrees of force, while at the same time lowering your pitch. Repeat the sentence several times, gradually increasing the amount of force applied until the volume has become louder, louder, and still louder while the pitch has remained the same. Repeat the sentence several more times, maintaining a consistent pitch and a resonant quality. With practice you should be able to control both the dgree of force in your voice and the level of pitch. This exercise should also help to make your phrasing more emphatic and improve your vocal energy.

Following are other suggestions that may prove valuble in achieving effective control and variety of volume.

- Learn to chart your volume as you might wish a listener to respond to it. If a recorder is available, especially one with a VU meter that has a visual indicator of the loudness level, tape your voice. Practice varying degrees of volume that could be used for pacing the significance and the forcefulness of words

Review the mechanics of the breathing process and make adequate use of exhaled breath that vibrates the vocal cords and amplifies the sound when singing. It is also beneficial to performance to have proper posture and an open stance when delivering songs to the audience. In *1776*, for example, the performers stand comfortably relaxed with the breathing mechanics of relaxation and projection ready to belt out a convincing song. (From the production of the University of Kansas. Stage direction by Jack B. Wright; musical direction by George Lawner; scenic and lighting design by David McGreevy; costume design by Delores Ringer; and choreography by Kristin Benjamin. Photography by Earl Iverson.)

read from a daily newspaper or a long speech from a musical.

- Suit your volume to the performance occasion and the size of the audience. Modify vocal characteristics accordingly, especially the degree of volume needed to overcome distractions.
- The degree with which force is suggested should be in proportion to the character's feelings and the desired audience response.
- Be aware of vocal fading, and avoid the tendency to trail off at the end of a line or song because of inadequate breath control.
- Be sensitive to audience reactions to volume and adjust the level accordingly.
- Learn to control the speed of your voice. It is very difficult to achieve forceful variety in volume if your rate is extremely fast or tediously slow.

Variety in volume also depends upon "performance sense." You should avoid the tendency to deliver parts of the speech or song at an unvarying level of loudness or softness for any imagined dramatic or spectacular effect. Remember that volume, or any of the other vocal variables, should be employed strategically for intelligent and purposeful performance.

QUALITY

Quality, or *vocal timbre*, is the specific characteristic of your voice that distinguishes it from any other voice of the same rate, pitch, or volume. As previously mentioned, the most common qualities are guttural, high-pitched, breathy, low-pitched, nasal, and "normal." Each of these qualities serves as a "vocal fingerprint" that helps to identify your individual tonal shade or color and to reveal your personality and attitude to the listener. For example, a noticeable lack of variety in quality might suggest that you have no energy or emotion or that you are uninterested and passive.

You may better understand the complexity of quality by reviewing its characteristic development in the description of resonation as part of the speech process. Recall that quality is influenced by the sound produced in the larynx by the vibration of the vocal cords, and that distinctive and expressive quality is the result of proper use of the resonation cavities. Recall, also, that the size, shape, and even texture of the resonating cavities determine the tonal variations necessary for a vital and vigorous voice.

To use variety in quality effectively, your normal timbre should be pleasing to the ear. That implies that your habitual quality is good and that you can subtly add variations or shadings to the voice by adjusting its timbre.

If you have a habitually unpleasant voice quality, however, you may need prolonged exercise and practice to improve upon basic weaknesses that impair meaningful performance. For example, permanent hoarseness may be the result of laryngitis, and it may be necessary to consult a speech pathologist for exercises or therapy to correct the huskiness. A consistently soft and thin quality of voice may be the result of poor breath support practiced through years of imitation of peers; it may be

necessary to learn and to practice daily the principles of diaphragmatic breathing that were described earlier.

When a weak vocal quality is more the result of neglect than of abuse, the following suggestions are made for improvement of tonal quality.

- Listen to sharpen your ear for changes in quality, and practice quality control by cultivating a "vocal vocabulary" of tones and shades of meaning.
- Maintain adequate breath support, and avoid strain on the voice by using your optimum level and pitch and a comfortable rate.
- Develop responsiveness in the voice by speaking and singing with animation and emotional honesty.
- Vowel sounds are the trademark of good quality, so practice producing vowel sounds that are crisp and clear.
- Review the production of quality in the resonation process, and work to free the throat, mouth, and nose of tension that might interfere with tonal variation and flexibility.

Practical application of the preceding discussion to a personal inventory of quality should indicate to you that it is essential to promote tonal variations and shades of vocal coloring as an effective means of providing the emphasis and personal expression necessary to gain listener attention.

SOME PRACTICAL
PERFORMANCE APPROACHES

As you prepare for musical theatre auditions, it would be wise to review the following suggestions. Begin with your music. Place all your selections in a looseleaf binder. Be sure that your music is in the correct key for your voice, whether it is in printed or manuscript form. All markings, corrections, and special notations should be clearly marked—boldly circled in red pen is a fine idea—so that your pianist can easily follow the score. Clearly mark first and second endings of music.

Consider the range of your musical repertoire for audition material. Your selections should take into account your vocal quality, vocal strengths and weaknesses, extremes of range, style, and ability to suggest character. The key to finding good material for auditions is maintaining an active file of songs that enhance your voice. Keep a notebook that catalogues songs in specific numbers appropriate for audition, such as ballads, character songs, comic songs, openings or closings, and narratives. Do include contemporary popular songs in your repertoire, and cultivate innovative changes in style, tempo, or interpretation to display your versatility and originality. It is also a good idea to watch for current recordings that might be appropriate audition material. Trade papers such as *Variety*, *Back Stage*, *Billboard*, and *Cashbox* list the top tunes in a variety of musical categories. Regardless of the source of your material, however, select only songs that are appropriate to your vocal range, allow you to sustain long notes, highlight your vocal versatility, provide interesting character interpretations, and enhance your vocal techniques. Following is a sample musical repertoire to guide you as you begin to collect your own audition material.

Opening/Closing Songs

"New York, New York"
"Cabaret"
"I Got Rhythm"
"Comedy Tonight"
"Everything's Coming Up Roses"
"That Old Black Magic"
"Another Op'nin', Another Show"
"Happily Ever After"
"On a Clear Day"
"There's No Business Like Show Business"
"People"
"Feeling Good"
"Who Can I Turn To (When Nobody Needs Me)"
"Come to the Ball"
"Hey, Look Me Over"

Comedy/Character Songs

"I Can't Say No"
"You Can't Get a Man with a Gun"
"I Got Rhythm"
"I Hate Men"
"I Won't Send Roses"
"Just You Wait"
"All Er Nothing"
"Mama, Look Sharp"
"Major General"
"I Wonder What the King Is Doing Tonight"
"Something Wonderful"
"Let's Call the Whole Thing Off"
"You Must Meet My Wife"
"My Heart Belongs to Daddy"
"On That Great Come-and-Get-It Day"
"The Man Who Got Away"

Narratives/Ballads

"The Trolley Song"
'Alfie"
"Pieces of Dreams"
"As Long as He Needs Me"
"Ballad of Frankie and Johnny"
"Goodnight, My Someone"
"I Loved You Once in Silence"
"The Party's Over"
"The Impossible Dream"
"Send in the Clowns"
"Summertime"
"What Kind of Fool Am I?"
"Donna"
"I Could Have Danced All Night"
"I Don't Know How to Love Him"
"The Name's LaGuardia"
"On the Street Where You Live"

Popular Songs

"All the Things You Are"
"Try to Remember"
"April in Paris"
"I Am My Own Best Friend"
"Let's Fall in Love"
"Can't Help Singing"
"Nothing Is Impossible"

"Be Happy"
"So in Love"
"A Foggy Day"
"Wish You Were Here"
"Lady, Be Good"
"Evergreen"
"I'll Take Romance"
"I Have the Love"

Rhythm/Blues Songs

"Stormy Weather"
"Hymn to Him"
"Ol' Man River"
"Is That All There Is?"
"Blues in the Night"
"That Old Black Magic"
"Without You"
"Love Isn't Born"
"Alone Too Long"
"The Party's Over"
"I'll Never Fall in Love Again"
"I'm Black"
"Bewitched, Bothered, and Bewildered"
"Yesterday"
"Be Happy"
"Someone in My Life"

OTHER CONSIDERATIONS

Auditions are an opportunity for you to present yourself in the best possible light and to emphasize your special skills. If you also play an instrument, tap dance, or perform a specialty act, you should be prepared to display those skills if asked to do so. In addition, your specific preparation for the audition should include the following perspectives.

- BE PREPARED

Poor preparation places you at a distinct disadvantage in the competitive audition. Rehearse your material well, and refrain from performing material that has not been solidly learned.

- BE POSITIVE

Approach the audition with the confidence that comes with positive preparation. Review your music to make sure it is in the proper key. Review your markings and notations to make sure they are appropriate for your voice. Review your instructions to the accompanist to make sure your material is clearly organized.

- BE PROFESSIONAL

Being professional in auditions means that you dress sensibly and highlight your best features by wearing what is appropriate and tasteful. Being professional means taking advantage of the opportunity to highlight yourself by moving gracefully, capturing the imagination of the moment, and displaying poise and energy.

- BE SENSIBLE

Being sensible means that you are prepared to accept either approval or disapproval. If you are not recommended for the role it could be the result of many factors: you may not physically fit the role, your voice may not be distinctive, or you may not fit the director's conception of the character. Auditions serve only to highlight your skills at a given moment, and do not always reveal your competence as a performer.

Of course, the more often you audition, the more likely you are to display poise, self-confidence, and maturity. Look at the audition as an opportunity to receive constructive criticism, and use the experience as a learning tool for other auditions to follow. Continue to seek professional evaluation from your peers, teachers, and vocal coaches; and continue to seek out public performance experiences that permit an audience to react to your presentation. All of these approaches to performance will provide you with a composite portrait of yourself as a performer and prepare you for later auditions that are memorable and exciting.

SUPPLEMENTARY EXERCISES

Although you cannot expect to discover a simple formula for predicting the degree of success you will have in musical performance, the guidelines and supplementary exercises provided in this chapter should give you an excellent foundation to support further development. What remains for you is disciplined rehearsal and critical review that will contribute to your growth and maturity as a musical performer.

ACT WITHOUT WORDS

Gestures are a necessary part of every musical theatre performance. They are generally defined as movements of any part of the body to help convey an idea or an emotion. They may include a raised eyebrow, a quick toss of the head, or a sweeping movement of the arms or hands. The primary aspect of gestures as they are used to reinforce and give added dimension to characterization is that they are motivated and natural. In the following examples of "acting without words," use gestures that help to define and clarify the action called for.

Begin by freeing yourself of the tension that inhibits natural gestures. (Listen to slow and melodious music and relax the body in a series of swaying motions like those described in "Poetry in Motion" in the exercises in Part I.) Remember, however, that every movement of the arms begins at the shoulders, passes through the elbow and the wrist, and "slips off" the ends of the fingers. Movements should also involve the entire body, and the wrist should lead in horizontal and vertical gestures.

Be sure to focus your attention on the *objects* and the *action* described below and to "see" and "feel" what is called for. Let your facial expressions reveal your reactions, and let your body respond to shapes, sizes, and weights as precisely as possible.

- Show a child of six the basics of playing baseball. Concentrate on the proper batting stance, the hitting of the ball, the running of the bases, and the reactions of the players.
- Stroll in a park and pick flowers, sit on a bench, read a newspaper, and then feed the pigeons popcorn. React to imaginary conversations with passersby and offer them objects that might be drawn from your pocket or handbag.
- Attend a public auction and bid on items that interest you. Inspect the glassware, the rare paintings, the furniture, and the books. Find yourself in a competitive bidding contest with a fellow patron who wants a unique silver goblet. React with appropriate facial expressions and gestures as the bidding reaches a point at which you can no longer compete.
- Stand in front of a mirror in a clothing store and try on hats, shirts, vests, pants, ties, and scarves. React to the fabric and the cut of the clothing. After careful consideration, select a hat, shirt, vest, and scarf and exit wearing them.
- Dine at an exclusive French restaurant, enhancing your meal with a bottle of rare wine. Order the specialty of the house and react to the sauce, the salad, the vegetables, the meat, and the dessert. Exhibit good table manners and appreciate the fine music being played.

Then discover that you have forgotten your wallet. Explain the problem in gestures to the waiter, who has not given you the best possible service.

THE MASKS OF EMOTION

The role of facial expressions is important in suggesting character mood and attitude. Musical theatre, in particular, demands flexible and pliable use of the face to help convey the masks of emotion needed in both dialogue and song. Begin the exercise by facing a full-length mirror at a distance of six feet. Observe your posture and face before proceeding: your body alignment, expressiveness of eyes, tilt of head, and poise. When you have an intimate understanding of how ''you'' look to others, cover your face with your hands.

The first mask to assume is that of *anger*. How will your facial expression and posture change to suggest this emotion? Will there be tension in the face? Will the body tense? Explore the mask of anger, slowly adjusting your facial expressions and posture to project it. Try to recapture the last experience you had with the emotion of anger. Concentrate on all the sensory impressions that were part

The role of facial expressions is an important one in helping you to suggest character mood and attitude. Musical theatre demands a flexible and pliable use of the face to help convey the masks of emotion needed to voice both dialogue and song. In this production of *OLIVER!* notice how active and informative facial expressions are in suggesting character mood and attitude. (From the production of Murray State University. Directed by Mark Malinauskas. Designed by Karen Boyd. Choreography by Beverly Rogers.)

of that experience, the situation, the tension, the sight, the smell, the taste, and even the sound involved. When you are comfortable with your mask of anger, drop your hands and observe yourself in the mirror. Is there a noticeable difference between the mask of anger and your previous posture and facial expression? Has your body adjusted its alignment to sugest the desired emotion? Have you altered your facial features significantly?

Now, cover your face again and produce the following masks of emotion, using the process outlined above. Continue to repeat the exercise until your facial expressions and posture capture the spirit of the suggested emotion.

- The mask of *love* for a dear friendenvy for another's possessions
- The mask of *despair* for being left alone
- The mask of *jealousy* for another's easy success
- The mask of *hope* for resolving a complicated problem
- The mask of *ecstasy* for a requited love
- The mask of *boredom* for the routine of life
- The mask of *respect* for a distinguished leader
- The mask of *bitterness* for a frustrated dream
- The mask of *repentance* for having made a mistake
- The mask of *resignation* for inevitable defeat

When you have developed a convincing adjustment in both facial expression and posture to suggest a desired attitude or mood, repeat the following excerpt from Edmond Rostand's *Cyrano de Bergerac*. Concentrate on incorporating as many of the masks of emotion as possible, but also add new masks that are suggested by the title character's changing point of view in the dialogue.

    Ah, no, young sir!
    You are too simple. Why, you might have
        said—
    Oh, a great many things! Mon dieu, why

waste your opportunity? For example,
    thus:—
AGGRESSIVE: I, sir, if that nose were mine,
    I'd have it amputated—on the spot!
FRIENDLY: How do you drink with such a
    nose?
You ought to have a cup made specially.
DESCRIPTIVE: 'Tis a rock—a crag—a
    cape—
A cape? say rather, a peninsula!
INQUISITIVE: What is that receptacle—
A razor-case or a portfolio?
KINDLY: Ah, do you love the little birds
So much that when they come and sing to
    you,
You give them this to perch on? INSOLENT:
Sir, when you smoke, the neighbors must
    suppose
Your chimney is on fire. CAUTIOUS: Take
    care—
A weight like that might make you topheavy.
THOUGHTFUL: Somebody fetch my
    parasol—
Those delicate colors fade so in the sun!
FAMILIAR: Well, old torchlight! Hang your
    hat
Over that chandelier—it hurts my eyes.
ELOQUENT: When it blows, the typhoon
    howls,
And the clouds darken. DRAMATIC: When
    it bleeds—
The Red Sea! ENTERPRISING: What a sign
For some perfumer! LYRIC: Hark—the horn
Of Roland calls to summon Charlemagne!—
SIMPLE: When do they unveil the monu-
    ment?
RESPECTFUL: Sir, I recognize in you
A man of parts, a man of prominence—
RUSTIC: Hey? What? Call that a nose? Na, na—
I be no fool like what you think I be—
That there's a blue cucumber! MILITARY:
Point against cavalry! PRACTICAL: Why not
A lottery with this for the grand prize?

Or—parodying Faustus in the play—
"Was this the nose that launched a thousand
    ships
And burned the topless towers of Ilium?"
These, my dear sir, are things you might have
    said
Had you some tinge of letters, or of wit
To color your discourse. But wit,—not so,
You never had an atom—and of letters,
You need but three to write you down—
    an ASS!

NOODLE SOUP

In developing awareness of movement in musical theatre, it is important to think of your body as an expressive instrument that conveys a visual portrait of self-confidence and relaxation. Graceful and fluid movements help to suggest poise and also communicate your coordination skills. Before attempting any movement exercises, you should be aware of your own sense of movement. Do you walk gracefully? Are your shoulders erect? Do you sometimes think you were born with "two left feet"? Can you follow the tempo of music? Once you have a sense of your own movement potential, you should be able to concentrate on specific weaknesses.

Begin this exercise by bending from your waist and touching your toes. Relax your arms in front of your feet and begin slowly to swing your head *and* your relaxed arms in a pendulum-like motion— as if you were a limp noodle in a pot of boiling water. Now begin to relax your legs and your chest cavity as you continue slowly to swing all parts of your body from side to side, finally collapsing in a soggy heap on the floor.

Next, lie flat on your back and slightly elevate your knees while keeping your feet flat on the floor. Be sure that your pelvis is tilted toward your knees and that your arms are flat on the floor at your sides. Inhale deeply for a count of 35; then exhale slowly for a count of 35. When all tension has been expelled from your chest cavity, *purr* like a playful kitten and sustain the sound for a count of 35, being sure that your throat is open and you are breathing comfortably.

Keeping your pelvis tilted toward your knees, continue to inhale deeply for a count of 35 and then slowly exhale for a count of 35 as you • *growl* like a dog • *hum* like a bird • *snort* like a horse • *buzz* like a bee • *whimper* like a puppy • *hiss* like a snake • *hoot* like an owl • *bray* like a mule • *squeak* like a mouse •and *crow* like a rooster. Next, stand up and let your body respond to the followinng movement suggestions. You may wish to play fifteen minutes of popular music to create spontaneous movement patterns that help to free your body from tension. If you use music, allow one minute for each movement suggested below.

- Move like a witch doctor exorcising evil spirits from a tribesman.
- Move like a burglar entering an empty house late at night.
- Move like a juggler performing on a crowded street corner.
- Move like an infantryman approaching the outskirts of an enemy post.
- Move like a magician executing an intricate trick.
- Move like a long-distance runner tiring near the finish line of a track meet.
- Move like a medieval king in mortal combat with his arch enemy.
- Move like a policeman directing rush-hour traffic.
- Move like a sophisticated fashion model displaying the latest Paris clothes.
- Move like a villain stealing slyly toward a beautiful heroine.
- Move like a circus clown riding a tricycle on an imaginary sheet of ice.
- Move like a dangerous criminal escaping from a maximum security prison late at night.

- Move like a mad scientist plotting to destroy the world with his plutonium bomb.
- Move like a tramp stumbling down a lonely country road.
- Move like an old maid sneaking into an X-rated movie.

"VOICING" MEANING

This performance exercise is structured in three parts to help you cultivate variety in your voice, which should be thought of as a musical instrument. The object of the exercise is to develop interpretation skills in reading literature while at the same time enhancing performance skills in *volume control, vocal variety,* and *pitch*. Although you should approach each part of the exercise as a separate unit, the concluding part integrates the individual skills into a unified whole.

I. To explore the role of volume control, take a full inhalation and voice the count of one very slowly, sustaining the *n* sound until all the air has been expelled from your lungs. Now take another full inhalation and voice the count of *two* very slowly, sustaining the *o* until all the air has been expelled from your lungs. Then, keeping your pitch consistent, count from 1 to 10 as you gradually increase your volume on each inhalation. Relax, and then reverse the sequence, beginning with a climactic voice count of 10 and gradually coming down to an almost whispered count of 1.

When you are confident that your volume control is flexible and that you can increase or decrease volume without changing pitch, voice the following excerpt from George Bernard Shaw's *Saint Joan*. Use volume control to highlight significant thoughts, making sure that you use as many levels of sound, from the whisper to the shout, as in the counting part of the exercise and that your pitch does not rise or fall as your volume changes.

If you command me to declare that all I have done and said, and all the visions and revela-tions I have had, were not from God, then that is impossible: I will not declare it for anything in the world. What God made me do I will never go back on; and what He has commanded or shall command I will not fail to do in spite of any man alive. That is what I mean by impossible. And in case the Church should bid me to do anything contrary to the command I have from God, I will not consent to it, no matter what it may be.

I believe that God is wiser than I; and it is His commands that I will do. All the things that you call crimes have come to me by the command of God: it is impossible for me to say anything else. If any Churchman says the contrary I shall not mind: I shall mind God alone, whose command I always follow.

II. To explore the role of vocal variety in performance, cultivate a *vocal vocabulary* of tones and shades of meaning, maintain adequate breath support to avoid strain on the voice, speak or sing at the optimum level of pitch using a comfortable rate, and produce vowel sounds that are crisp and clear. Frequent repetition of the following voice exercises should help you improve your vocal gymnastics and also promote self-confidence and poise. Undertake each exercise with intensity, working actively to free the throat, mouth, and nose of any tension that might interfere with the development of tonal variation and vocal variety.

JUMPING JAW: To cultivate a relaxed jaw that will enable you to speak or sing fluently and clearly, let your head fall slowly toward your chest. Rotate your head up and down, keeping the jaw relaxed. Slowly roll your head toward the right and then toward the left, making a semicircle with your head motions. Now relax and place your hands on your cheekbones as you slowly lift your head upward, keeping the jaw relaxed and motionless. When your head is finally lifted, the jaw should sag open. With the jaw relaxed and open, repeat the following phrases, moving only the tip of your tongue: *da-da-da-da, de-de-de-de, la-la-la-la,* and *le-le-le-le*. Repeat 10 times, or until your jaw begins to tense.

B. *DEEP THROAT:* To cultivate an open throat that will enable you to speak in a relaxed and conversational tone, yawn deeply as you take sustained breaths for a count of 20. Slowly exhale and repeat the following sounds as you relax your jaw to give voice to rounded and full vowels: *da-da-da-da, de-de-de-de, le-le-le-le, la-la-la-la, le-le-le-le-leap, la-la-la-lamp.* Repeat 10 times, increasing volume with each repetition.

C. *LOOSE LIPS:* To cultivate flexible lips that will enable you to sing distinctly and precisely, open your mouth wide to form an *O*. Keep your tongue flat in your mouth as you rest the tip of your tongue at the ridge of your lower teeth. Alternating your lips from a small *O* to a large *O*, repeat the following sounds in short bursts of breath: *oh-oh-oh-oh, ah-ah-ah-ah, mo-mo-mo-mo,* and *no-no-no-no.* Repeat 10 times, keeping your lips rounded and your tongue flat.

D. *TRILLING TONGUE:* To cultivate a tongue that "trills" *d*'s, *t*'s, and *ing*'s to enable you to speak and sing fluidly and flexibly, slowly arch your tongue toward the roof of your mouth as you rapidly repeat the following sounds: *d-d-d-d-don't, t-t-t-t-teeth,* and *s-s-s-s-sing.* Now "trill" the following phrases as you emphasize each *d, t,* and *ing* as precisely as possible: *dentist, don't, teacher, laughing, tight, disappoint, running,* and *distant.* Repeat 10 times, arching your tongue to pronounce words distinctly.

When you have completed these preliminary exercises, you are ready to first speak and then sing the following passage from Louise Saunder's *POOR MADDALENA* free of vocal tension and strain. First, speak the passage, paying particular attention to the way your throat and mouth change shape and size to form sound, and striving to keep your breathing relaxed and natural. Second, sing the passage to the tune of a popular song as you cultivate an open throat, a relaxed jaw, flexible lips, and a "trilling" tone.

> I see a great heap of gold, mountain-high. Men are crawling over it, clutching it, and slipping down. At its base there is a dark crowd of people, scrambling, fighting, grabbing one another. But near the top there are not so many. They climb more easily. I see a temple with shadowy columns reaching to the sky, but it is empty—no, not quite. Just then I saw a man leave the temple and join the others at the mountain of gold. And look—there goes another. He is running—and yet another! Yes, but there are still men left in the temple. I can see them now. Listen, they are singing. Oh, what music? Do you hear?

III. To explore the role of pitch in performance, you need to discover your optimum pitch level. The optimum pitch level is where your voice falls on the musical scale, and it is an indication of the range of which your voice is capable. To discover your optimum pitch level, block yours ears with your fingers and reach for a comfortable high note, then slowly sing down the scale to a comfortable low note; conclude by singing up *and* down the musical scale. When you have heard the musical note that sounds the loudest to you, that note is your optimum pitch.

When you have isolated your pitch, voice the following excerpt from Arthur Miller's *The Price*. First maintain your optimum pitch level, but then emphasize significant words or phrases by singing up and down the scale. Repeat the exercise 10 times, or until you increase your pitch range potential. Remember, however, that hoarseness or vocal fatigue may follow if you overdo this part of the exercise. If you feel signs of vocal strain, stop and relax. Practice for five minutes as a start and gradually increase to eight minutes.

> You wanted a real life. And that's an expensive thing; it costs. I know I may sound terribly naive, but I'm still unused to talking about anything that matters. Frankly, I didn't answer your calls this week because I was afraid. I've struggled so long for a concept of myself and I'm not sure I can make it believable to you. But I'd like to. You see, I got to a certain point where…I dreaded my own work; I finally couldn't cut it. There are times, as you know, when if you leave someone alone he might live a year or two; while if you go in you might kill him. I ran into a cluster of misjudgments. It can happen, but it never had to me, not one on top of the other. And they all had one thing in common; they'd all been diagnosed by other men as inoperable. Why had I taken risks that very competent men had declined? And the quick answer, of course, ĭs—to pull off the impossible. Shame the competition. But suddenly I saw something else. And it was terror. In dead center, directing my brains, my hands, my ambition—for thirty years.

Now that you have mastered the three parts of the exercise as separate units, it is time to integrate the skills of volume control, vocal variety, and pitch into a unified whole. As you voice the following excerpt from Henrik Ibsen's *Peer Gynt*, try to (a) increase or decrease your volume without changing pitch; (b) try to add vocal tones and shades of meaning to the speech; (c) cultivate your optimum pitch; and (d) maintain the general characteristics of ''jumping jaw,'' ''deep throat,'' ''loose lips,'' and ''trilling tongue.'' You might wish to tape record this part of the exercise for future reference.

> Silence! Did my beauty listen?
> What did she think of my little song?
> Is she peeping behind the curtain,
> Stripped of her veils and everything?
> What's that? Sounds like somebody tore
> A cork from a bottle violently!
> Again? And again! What could it be?
> Sighs, perhaps? Love's melody—
> No, that was a definite snore—
> Sweetest music! Anitra sleeps.
> Nightingale, be muted now!
> You'll get your money's worth in woe
> If you dare mingle your raucous pipes—
> Oh well, as the book says, let it go!
> The nightingale is a troubadour;
> And, for all that, so am I.
> Both of us with our music snare
> Hearts that are tender, mild, and shy.
> The cool of night is made for singing;
> Song defines our common role.
> Song is our way of remaining
> *Us*, Peer Gynt and the nightingale.
> And just this, my beauty there asleep,
> No more; only to touch my lip
> To the cup, and leave the nectar safe—
> But look, she's coming out at last!
> Well, after all, that is the best.

WHOSE BUSINESS IS THIS, ANYWAY?

Characterization is not merely a matter of memorizing dialogue or being familiar with song lyrics; it also involves the skillful handling of *props* and *stage business*. Props, which may include eyeglasses, lighter, fan, umbrella, or handkerchief, are usually small objects held in the hand and used to punctuate or underscore dialogue, song, or action. Props may also help to define a character's behavior or to illuminate subtext. Stage business, which may include reading a book, smoking a cigarette, taking a pratfall, looking into a mirror, or eating a meal, is usually a means of conveying an attitude or suggesting a character's primary activity in a scene. Stage business may also help to define character motivation or shades of intent.

In the exercise that follows, respond to the scene by supplying appropriate hand props and stage business that permit you not only to "do" but also to "speak" or "sing" while doing. Memorize the following selection from Molière's *The Miser* so that you are free to use props and to create stage business without use of the script:

> Sir, I'll tell you frankly they make fun of you all over town; from every quarter they toss a hundred jibes at us, all about you. One of them says you have special calendars printed, in which Lent and the days of penitence are doubled, so as to profit by the fasting you force on your household. Another says you always keep in reserve something to blame on your servants when the holidays come round, or when they leave your service so you will have a reason for giving them no tips.

> Still another tells a story about how you once had the cat of one of your neighbors supoenaed because it had eaten a left-over scrap of mutton chop which belonged to you. Another tells how you were taken by surprise one night as you were coming yourself to steal the oats of your own horses, and how your coachman, the one before me, gave you, in the darkness, I don't know how many whacks with a stick—about which you kept quiet. In short—do you want me to tell you?—one cannot go anywhere without hearing you being taken to pieces. You are the talk and the butt of the whole town, and they never mention you except in terms of miser, pinch-penny, and sordid skinflint.

Conclude the exercise by using appropriate props and stage business to create the following improvised scenes. Again, concentrate on voicing the memorized selection so that you not only "do" but also "speak" while doing. When you have finished the last suggested scene, you might wish to expand the exercise by "singing" the dialogue and incorporating imaginative stage movement into your use of props and stage business. You might also wish to tape record the final dialogue as a prelude to the later exercises that are concerned with using the musical voice in characterization.

- Setting an elaborate dinner table for a formal party
- Waiting on tables in an elegant restaurant
- Dressing to go dancing at a disco
- Intently watching an exciting football game
- Working a difficult crossword puzzle
- Cleaning a disorderly living room
- Attending a solemn family reunion
- Riding a noisy subway train
- Shopping in a supermarket
- Working as as security guard

ONE DAY AT A TIME

To guide your performance preparation further, you may wish to incorporate the following rehearsal schedule in your routine. With the relaxation, poise, and self-confidence that may be gained by following a daily schedule of vocal and physical exercises, you should be able to meet the demands of any performance situation. If you are able to set aside at least 30 minutes a day for practice and rehearsal, you should notice a marked improvement in both your vocal and bodily technique.

I. Body Exercises: 10-minute sequence
   a. Stretch arms and legs
   b. Bend shoulders and knees
   c. Rotate head and neck
   d. Rotate torso and legs
   e. Execute 5 push-ups
   f. Execute 5 jumping-jacks
   g. Conclude by jogging in a circle

II. Limbering-up Exercises: 10-minute sequence
   a. Rotate hands and arms
   b. Rotate torso and legs
   c. Rotate each finger
   d. Rotate each toe
   e. Rotate head and neck
   f. Rotate jaws and fists
   g. Conclude by jogging in a circle

III. Vocal Relaxation Exercises:
   10-minute sequence

   a. Rotate neck and jaw
   b. Pant heavily
   c. Sob quietly
   d. Babble incoherently
   e. Chant lightly
   f. Count to 20 on one breath
   g. Voice a tongue-twister or jingle
   h. Conclude by jogging in a circle

When you have completed the daily schedule of exercises, you may wish to evaluate your degree of vocal and physical relaxation by reciting the following excerpt from Edmond Rostand's *Cyrano de Bergerac*. You should appear natural and relaxed, with posture erect, bones of the body in proper alignment, hands at the sides, and voice free of tension. Your legs should be spread slightly apart, the weight of the body should fall evenly upon the feet, and the voice should be energetic.

My old friend—look at me,
And tell me how much hope remains for me
With this protuberance! Oh, I have no more
Illusions! Now and then—bah! I may grow
Tender, walking alone in the blue cool
Of evening, through some garden fresh
   with flowers
After the benediction of the rain;
My poor big devil of a nose inhales
April...and so I follow with my eyes
Where some boy, with a girl upon his arm,
Passes a patch of silver...and I feel
Somehow, I wish I had a woman too,
Walking with little steps under the moon,
And holding my arm so, and smiling. Then
I dream—and I forget...
   And then I see
The shadow of my profile on the wall!

Part III

DIRECTING
THE MUSICAL

DIRECTING THE MUSICAL

The director of musical theatre in the nonprofessional area will, more than likely, wear a variety of hats. The nature of amateur theatre is such that the director of a production may serve as producer, choreographer, and, on occasion, designer of sets, lights, and costumes. "Director" is such a broad title that it is necessary to separate and define the tasks that are strictly directorial (and choreographic) from those that would normally be done by the producer. (If the director is indeed also producer and choreographer, one can only wish him or her energy!)

The approach to directing the musical discussed here is based on a seemingly simple premise: directing is directing! Directing a musical comedy is not essentially different from directing a play by Shakespeare or one by Tennessee Williams. *A Funny Thing Happened on the Way to the Forum* and *A Streetcar Named Desire* share more similarities than differences. True, the intended audience response is different, the styles of the shows are drastically opposite, and the demands placed upon the actors are not the same at all. Yet each is a single dramatic action communicated by a group of actors to an audience. Each production is, simply, a piece of theatre.

The primary difference between the two plays is the form that each takes: *Forum* expresses conflict, character action, and strong feeling through singing and dancing in a modernized version of ancient Rome; *Streetcar* does the same by recreating a naturalistic sense of life in New Orleans in the early 1950's.

Focusing on the similarities between musical and nonmusical theatre forces us as directors to view a musical work as a piece of legitimate theatre, to discover the conflicts, actions, circumstances that contribute to the creation of this particular musical's

"reality." Ignoring the similarities and seeing musical comedy as an "illegitimate" child of "real theatre" poses problems for the director. The essence of theatre disappears and is replaced by singing and dancing automatons who have no clue as to why they are singing and dancing. The outer shell of the form may be present, but there is no heart to the production. Clearly, musical theatre is a heightened form of theatre, one in which characters reach such a high pitch of emotion that the only form of expression available is a song or a dance. It is interesting to note that this is sometimes the case in "real life" as well.

Thus, the director of a musical is faced with the same set of tasks that confront the director of any play:

- Choosing a show
- Holding auditions and casting the show
- Completing character and script analyses
- Establishing a rehearsal schedule and planning rehearsal activity
- Determining use of space and the overall visual design of the show
- Handling movement and dance if a choreographer is not present
- Communicating with actors throughout the rehearsal and production process
- Communicating with other production personnel: the technical and design staff and the producer

In short, the director is a decision-maker and a facilitator when working on a musical, much as he or she is when approaching a nonmusical work. Each of the above tasks is discussed in more detail later in this chapter.

CHOOSING THE MUSICAL

For the director working today, literally hundreds of musicals are available. In any theatrical setting, a number of factors influence the choice of musical to be mounted:

1. Cost of the musical—royalty fees as well as the cost of producing the show (sets, costumes).
2. Size of cast and availability of actors, singers, and dancers.
3. Audience appeal given the community in which the show is to be presented.
4. Time available for rehearsal and production work.

Depending on the nature of the theatrical organization, there may be additional considerations. Given the wide variety of musicals available—large cast, small cast; heavy dance, light dance; serious, comic; complex musical score, simple orchestration; all styles and periods—there is bound to be one to suit every director's circumstances.

Regardless of financial and technical considerations, it is important for the director to choose a musical with a concept or vision of the show in mind. The "why" of the production needs to be artistic as well as financial or technical. The director ought to like the play, see its potential, feel that it says something to him or her. A strong artistic point of view regarding the show is crucial when the director begins to consider the basic production approach and focuses on cuts or changes in the script. Decisions whether to add singers or dancers to a chorus, to delete songs or dances, to combine or eliminate characters, or to change the setting should be the result of the director's vision of the musical. For example, in a production of *The Fantasticks* the director, in an effort to underscore her point of view about the romantic conflicts of the play, cast not one but two actors as Mutes, one male and one female. In several scenes, the Mute couple assumed greater dramatic importance as they were able to mirror or shadow the activities of the lovers Matt and Luisa as they fell in love, then out, and finally back into love again. The addition of the extra Mute provided a different approach or artistic perspective on the romantic aspects of the show.

CASTING THE SHOW

Considerations

Once the musical has been chosen, possibly in conjunction with other artistic personnel—musical director, choreographer, designers—the next area of decision-making is auditioning and casting. Long before this process actually begins, the production staff—director, choreographer, and musical director—will have held many discussions regarding the requirements of the show and its cast demands in all three areas: acting, singing, and dancing. Some musicals require that the performers have all three skills; others focus on each performer's ability in a single area. *West Side Story* requires an ensemble that dances extremely well but, if need be, may sing only adequately. *A Funny Thing Happened on the Way to the Forum* requires two male principals, Pseudolus and Hysterium, who are accomplished comic actors, whereas *Pippin*'s Lead Player must be the proverbial "triple threat" as the character drives the production forward by his extraordinary acting, singing, and dancing. The production staff needs to consider the following questions:

1. Are there either principal roles or ensembles that rely completely on singing and/or dancing?
2. What is the range of the vocal score and the vocal range of individual characters?
3. Must some characters be much better actors than they are singers or dancers?
4. Are specialty dancers needed (*i.e.*, tap)?
5. Is the choreography (or could it be) stylized movement rather than formal dancing?

Once these general considerations have been noted, the director needs to study the demands of the individual characters with regard to physical type, age, and quality.

Physical Type. The professional theatre generally pays more attention to the physical nature of the person auditioning than does the nonprofessional theatre, often out of sheer necessity. It is not uncommon for a professional actor to walk into an audition, be looked over by the director or an assistant, and be dismissed as the wrong type: too heavy, too light; too tall, too short; wrong coloring. "Typing out" is a luxury the amateur theatre can seldom afford. Although the director needs to be aware of the visual or physical requirements of a character, there are ways of compensating for physical "defects": casting a short ensemble around a short leading man to make him look taller; casting a tall male principal to make a tall female principal appear more average in height. At times casting against suggested physical type can be a bonus as well as a necessity. Problems arise in casting a nonprofessional musical to mirror the Broadway production of the show. Pseudolus, the wickedly funny slave who longs to be free in *A Funny Thing Happened on the Way to the Forum*, is often cast as the Zero Mostel type, since he originated the role on Broadway. However, casting a tall (or short), thin (rather than heavy), younger (rather than older) male in this role may contribute to the cunning and comedy of the character without harming the play in the slightest.

Age. In nonprofessional theatre, actors are often cast in roles far outside their own age range. This is particularly true at the high school level, where no actors are actually in the middle-aged range. Nevertheless, even in school settings some actors project an age much older than their actual age, whereas some students can comfortably and believably play much younger than their age. A certain level of audience acceptance can be expected when viewing nonprofessional theatre. However, the director should, as much as possible, cast with age in mind and avoid glaring differences among cast members such as casting a "mother" who appears much younger than her "daughter."

Quality. Finally, the director needs to consider the overall emotional or psychological quality or feeling associated with the character. Can this actor play a gentle, sweet, naïve ingenue? Can that actor master the role of a street tough, hardened by life? This is a fairly subjective area unless the director has seen the actor's work previously, and often the director must rely on directorial instinct.

Any one of these three areas—physical type, age, quality—may be more important than the others in a given script, and this, too, should be noted by the director.

Audition Procedure

The audition process itself needs to be as well organized as possible. Clearly, having casting or rehearsal assistants is most helpful, particularly if the director is also serving as choreographer. Assuming that actors are not simply rejected by type before the audition begins, at a minimum the director, musical director, and choreographer need to have the actor read, sing, and dance.

The audition can be handled in a variety of ways. Some directors choose to interview actors individually before the audition. Most often in nonprofessional theatre, actors simply answer the open call at a designated time and are informed where to go and when. At this time, the actors usually fill out an audition form. The "form" may be a 3 x 5 card requesting name, address, and phone number, or it may be a sheet calling for additional information.

The audition process may be outlined as follows:

AUDITION SHEET FOR
A MUSICAL PRODUCTION

Name _____

Address_____Phone_____(Home)

_____   _____(School)

Vocal Range _____

Dance/Movement Experience or Training _____

_____

Role interested in _____

Would you accept any role? _____

Evening or weekend commitments between now and October 26:

Please do not write below this line.

_____

1. Actors read a prepared two-minute monologue and/or cutting from the musical; they are given a few minutes to glance at the scene.
2. Actors then sing either prepared material or something from the show, as requested by the musical director. In professional settings, 16 bars of music (sometimes less) is usually sufficient to permit the musical director to appraise skill; in academic settings actors often sing a complete number.
3. If the choreographer is not the director, the actors may then be requested to move to a different location to work with the choreographer. Usually the choreographer gives the actors a combination of steps related to the style of the show and works with them in relatively small groups—six to fifteen, depending on the choreographer's preference and the number of auditionees. If the director is also serving as choreographer, a ''dance captain'' or assistant choreographer might work with actors in a separate location before having the director/choreographer view their dance auditions.

Following all auditions, and callbacks if necessary, the production staff discusses the final casting decisions with the director. At this point it is important to review the prior discussions regarding specific casting requirements of principals and chorus.

SCRIPT AND CHARACTER ANALYSIS

A thorough analysis of the script, including songs and dances and their placement in the show, and the characters is necessary in order to achieve crea-

tive and smooth-running rehearsals. At a minimum the director should determine the following:

1. The central or overriding action of the musical. What, essentially, is the show about? Choosing a central action will help the director shape scenes and give a proper perspective to songs and dances. Is _West Side Story_ a play about gang survival and warfare in the streets of New York city or a commentary on thwarted love in a dangerous environment? Your answer will make a difference in the focus and direction of certain scenes.
2. The central or primary conflict(s) in the show. Decide where, when, and how the major character clashes occur in the script. Is the central conflict of _West Side Story_ the New York gangs vs. the New York policemen, or the clash of cultures, territories, and ways of life as embodied by the two gangs?
3. The circumstances of the musical. Clarifying the environmental situation provides insight into character behavior. The geographical location, the time of the action, the economic, political, and social conditions surrounding the show are all factors that will affect the director's decisions with regard to character interaction. The musical _Cabaret_ is clearly a show of prewar Germany; any attempt to stage it requires an understanding of the social and economic circumstances of Hitler's Germany of the late 1930's.
4. Previous action. The director needs to specify all events prior to the play's beginning that will affect the current action. It is significant that the rival gangs of _West Side Story_, the Jets and the Sharks, have had battles long before the play's opening chords.

CHARACTER ANALYSIS

Detailed work on both principal characters and chorus members should yield a quantity of information that is usable for both director and actors.

Character Objectives. Ascertain each character's

primary objective or goal throughout the course of the production:

- What does each character want (*objective*)?
- What prevents the character from obtaining that objective (*obstacle*)?
- What does the character do to obtain what he or she wants (*action*)?

This triangle of character behavior—objective, obstacle, action—is the impetus for all of the activity in the play: It drives the central action forward. For example, the two fathers in *The Fantasticks* want their children to marry each other. The obstacle is the young couple: Children never do what their parents wish them to do. Thus the fathers are forced into action: the creation of a fake abduction and phony heroics, which fuels the remainder of the musical.

The Inner Character. Each actor will naturally explore the inner life of his or her character. It is necessary for the director to have a good grasp of each character as well. Doubtless there will be detail that only the actor can supply, but the bold strokes of characterization should be agreed upon by both director and actor.

The inner character includes the individual's philosophy of life and beliefs as well as personality. Much of this information is derived from the character's background and helps create a general psychological profile from which the actor can develop an elaborate characterization. The inner character analysis will aid the director's and the actor's understanding of the character's objectives,

The triangle of character behavior—*objective, obstacle,* and *action*—is the impetus for all the activity in the play. It drives the central action of the musical forward. In *ONCE UPON A MATTRESS*, for example, the characters visualize their character behavior to help clearly define their attitudes. (From the production of the University of Minnesota. Directed and choreographed by Peter Jablonski. Scenery, props, costume, and lighting design by Scott Donaldson.)

which, in turn, makes character actions more specific and detailed.

The Outer Character. What does each character look like? As suggested earlier, the director may not have the luxury of casting actors to fit exactly the mental image created. Yet it is crucial to note the physical characteristics of each character as indicated in the script. Whether the character has blond or brown hair may not be important. However, a handicap or an ailment; the way he or she must walk or sit; posture, gestures, and the way he or she wears clothes will affect the performance. The inner character necessarily has an effect on the outer character and vice versa.

To begin the discovery process of each character's inner life and outer form, answer the following questions and keep a detailed account of all information gathered:

- What is my purpose in the play?
- How did I get into these circumstances?
- With whom am I in conflict?
- How do I reveal the conflict?
- What are my primary objectives, obstacles, and actions?
- What are the dominating desires of the other characters with whom I come in contact?
- What is my background?
- What surroundings do I live in?
- What is my social position? Financial standing?
- What is my family like?
- What are my typical bearing, posture, mannerisms, habits?
- What is my age?
- What kind of voice do I have?
- What type of clothing do I wear?
- How is my health?
- Have I had any recent experiences that would be reflected physically?
- What is my personality?
- How do I see myself? How do others see me?
- What kinds of emotions do I experience?
- Am I changeable?

One final note on the subject of character analysis. It is sometimes easy when directing a musical—indeed, when directing any large-cast play with many minor characters or "walk-ons"—to lump all members of the chorus together and view them in a general sense: townspeople, ladies and gentlemen of the court, slaves, or members of a gang. This tends to produce generalized performances that lack the impact created by a group of individuals rather than a group of townspeople. The director may not produce character profiles for each member of the chorus, but it is wise to encourage chorus members to do this work themselves: What do they want? Why are they present? What obstacles do they face? Many directors and actors actually assign created names and backgrounds to members of the ensemble in order to give their performances more substance. Nothing could speak more directly to this point than *A Chorus Line*. Once having heard the individuals speak about the joys and sorrows of their lives, it is difficult to imagine the chorus as a generic group of singers and dancers!

REHEARSAL PROCESS

From the beginning of the rehearsal period it is wise to keep a rehearsal journal as a complete record of the process. Such a log, an objective description of rehearsal activity and a candid appraisal of progress, will assist the director by providing an ongoing point of reference from which to approach rehearsal problems. The journal will also provide an opportunity for postshow evaluation.

Preparation

After the script analysis and discussion among the members of the production staff and before meeting the cast, the director should create the prompt book, which serves as a visual record of the production. The standard format calls for a copy of the ground plan facing every page of script, thus allowing space for notations on blocking, character activity, sets and props, and any other area of the

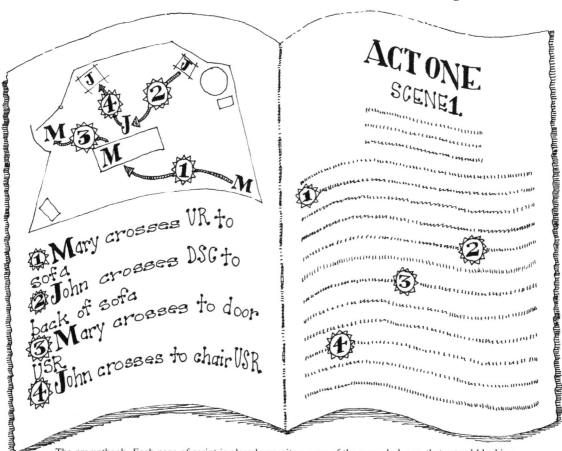

The promptbook. Each page of script is placed opposite a copy of the ground plan so that actors' blocking can be noted.

production that the director finds appropriate. The prompt book should include the character analyses, any research notes, and the rehearsal journal.

The script of the musical needs to be broken down into *beats*, or units within each scene. A beat is considered the smallest actable segment of the script. A new beat occurs every time there is a change in the action. Changes may be caused by the entrance or exit of a character, a shift in the topic of conversation or a character's motivation, or an adjustment in the through line of the action. These beats need to be clearly marked and are the basis for the rehearsal process. Working beat by beat, whether song, dance, or dialogue, permits the director to attend to the detail of character action and motivation. When a beat has been rehearsed, several of these building blocks may be put together

into a sequence and rehearsed until whole scenes and, finally, acts are complete.

Rehearsal Schedule

The second primary task facing the director before he or she faces the cast is the scheduling of rehearsal time. This is a crucial matter and one that must be worked out carefully in conjunction with the choreographer and the musical director. It requires that all three personnel dissect the musical and determine the proportion of songs to dances to nonmusical segments that exist in the script. Some musicals are really a series of songs and dances loosely connected by brief scenes of dialogue. *Dames at Sea* is one such musical. Others such as *Cabaret* have much more complicated plots and character interactions. Some musicals feature relatively small casts and few principals in the musical numbers. Below is a breakdown of the musical numbers in *Dames at Sea*; notice that most of the songs are handled by the five principals:

Act One

"Wall Street"	Mona
"It's You"	Dick and Ruby
"Broadway Baby"	Dick
"That Mister Man of Mine"	Mona and Chorus
"Choo-Choo Honeymoon"	Joan and Lucky
"The Sailor of My Dreams"	Ruby
"Singapore Sue"	Lucky and Company
"Good Times Are	
"Here to Stay"	Joan and Company

Act Two

"Dames at Sea"	Company
"The Beguine"	Mona and Captain
"Raining in My Heart"	Ruby and Chorus
"There's Something About You"	Dick and Ruby
"Raining in My Heart" (Reprise)	Ruby
"The Echo Waltz"	Mona, Joan, Ruby & Company
"Star Tar"	Ruby and Chorus
"Let's Have a Simple Wedding"	Company

Musicals such as *Fiddler on the Roof, Oklahoma!, Carousel,* and *Man of La Mancha* have larger casts featuring very active choruses; the singing and dancing is done by a wider variety of characters. Regardless of the size of the cast or the complexity of the musical component, time should be organized thoughtfully so that "waiting time" is minimized. When drawing up the rehearsal schedule consider the following possibilities:

1. Actors with primary singing responsibilities (solo or duet) might rehearse with the musical director outside the established rehearsal period; the same holds true for dance numbers that are solo or duet or of a specialty nature.
2. Chorus song and dance rehearsals may be scheduled opposite principal nonmusical scenes, thus making rehearsal time more ef-

ficient. This simultaneous rehearsing requires a separate choreographer or competent dance captain and a separate musical director.
3. After working smaller segments or beats of a scene without music, it is wise to run larger sections of the script with song and dance included in order to provide an overview of the show for all those involved.

On the facing page is a sample rehearsal schedule for *Dames at Sea*, covering a typical six-week period.

Weeks five and six are devoted primarily to polishing the show and handling technical considerations.

Rehearsals may be scheduled to accomplish work at a faster or slower pace, depending on the availability of time and the abilities of the cast. The sample schedule given here is the cumulative rehearsal model, in which each rehearsal builds upon the one before. It may prove more profitable for the director to schedule all choreography for the first week or two of rehearsal and reserve staging and working of nonmusical sequences for the later weeks.

Process

A glance at the sample schedule suggests that there are several types of rehearsals that the director will encounter while preparing the musical for presentation:

1. Rehearsals devoted primarily to the choreography of the musical numbers.
2. Rehearsals intended for the staging and working of nonmusical sequences and musical segments for character interaction, developing the dramatic action of the play by composition and movement, and devising business with props and set pieces.
3. Running sequences of the script or whole scenes or Acts.
4. Polishing the show and running technical rehearsals.

Rehearsal Schedule for Dames at Sea

Week	Rehearsal	Activity
I	1	Read, sing through the script.
	2	Choreograph "Wall Street," "It's You," and "Broadway Baby."
	3	Stage pages 5–12; work songs and dances.
	4	Choreograph "That Mister Man of Mine," "Choo-Choo Honeymoon," and "The Sailor of My Dreams."
	5	Stage pages 12–19; work songs and dances.
II	1	Work scene 1: pages 5–19, including first six songs.
	2	Choreograph "Singapore Sue" and "Good Times Are Here to Stay."
	3	Stage pages 20–30; work scene 2.
	4	Run Act One.
	5	Choreograph "Dames at Sea" and "The Beguine."
III	1	Stage pages 31–37; work songs and dances.
	2	Choreograph "Raining in My Heart," "There's Something About You," and "Raining in My Heart" (Reprise)
	3	Stage pages 37–42; work songs and dances.
	4	Work scene 1: pages 31–42.
	5	Choreograph "The Echo Waltz" and "Star Tar."
IV	1	Choreograph "Let's Have a Simple Wedding" and stage pages 43–52.
	2	Run Act Two.
	3	Work Act One.
	4	Work Act Two.
	5	Run Acts One and Two.

The following discussion deals with each type of rehearsal in greater detail.

First Meeting. The first rehearsal is intended to provide an overview of the show to the entire cast and production staff. Actors read the script and the musical director or rehearsal accompanist may play and/or sing through the musical numbers. The director gets a sense of the actors who have been cast, and the actors get a clear sense of how their characters fit into the show. It is helpful for the musical director and the choreographer to attend the first rehearsal so that they, too, get a feel for the production. Having everyone involved in the production present at this meeting tends to create a positive working environment. At this time, the director may choose to discuss the musical, its characters, conflicts, and ideas; the period of the play, or other pertinent information. He or she may, however, wish to reserve this discussion for later rehearsals.

Choreography of Musical Numbers. These rehearsals are usually run by the choreographer. However, the director may also be functioning as the choreographer or may be staging simple movement for some musical numbers. Since the next section is devoted to choreography, we shall postpone further discussion of this type of rehearsal. A final note, however, is important. There may be many moments when choreographing and working rehearsals are run simultaneously. The choreographer may work with the chorus while the director works with principal actors. For example, the director could stage nonmusical segments with Dick, Ruby,

Lucky, and Joan while the choreographer stages a number with Mona and the Chorus.

Working Rehearsals. The director's objective during all rehearsals is to set up as creative an environment as possible to free the actors to do their work. The specific demands of choreographic rehearsals at which the actors must learn dances by rote of necessity create a very structured, nonspontaneous atmosphere.

Working rehearsals by their very nature permit a free, creative approach to the material. The key to productive working rehearsals is the development of an improvisational atmosphere: not a chaotic, pointless waste of time, but a structured, creative discovery process. Improvisation, as used here, suggests a process that is organic, one that grows naturally from the actor's work with the script rather than being derived from the imposition of ideas on the actors and the script. The rehearsal objectives are as follows:

- To discover and develop moment-by-moment character action and interaction.
- To dramatize visually the central action and central conflicts of the script.
- To integrate the songs and dances so that they grow from the moments preceding them and generate the moments following them.

All rehearsals are working rehearsals in the sense that every moment of rehearsal time ought to contribute to the discovery process. The activities suggested below, though of primary value during working rehearsals, are also useful during choreographing, running, and polishing rehearsals. The improvisational approach to the rehearsal process might include some of the following exercises as bases for the development of characterization and dramatic action:

1. Reread the show or segments of the show and reverse roles between two characters or switch roles among several characters. This provides actors with different points of view on their own and other characters.

2. Improvise movement around a ground plan, either the actual ground plan or one similar to it. This offers an opportunity to visualize character relationships and to develop dramatic action. Experimenting with various ground plans may generate different aspects of character interaction.

3. Improvise moments in the script or create scenes outside the script for characters to develop. This permits actors to discover characters' subtext and motivation.

4. Improvise moments and scenes around the conflicts of the script so that individual actors place their character within the context of the musical's conflicts.

5. Improvise moments or actions understood to have happened before the show begins. This deepens the actor's understanding of characters' relationships and motivations.

6. Place characters in settings different from those of the script and improvise solutions to problems. This broadens the actor's sense of character.

7. Paraphrase lines to help the actors understand the text.

8. Create and improvise interior monologues to help actors to understand the subtext, or meaning "below" the lines. In this exercise, actors softly voice their feelings and thoughts about events taking place on the stage in a nonstop, stream-of-consciousness manner. At appropriate moments, they supply their lines in full voice to maintain the progress of the play. This exercise demands great concentration and commitment.

9. Create character biographies to help actors fill in the details of their characterizations. This is especially important for characters about whom little information is provided in the script.

10. Improvise with actual or substituted props. The presence of realistic objects may trigger the actor's imagination, and this creativity may generate interesting and inventive business.

11. During rehearsals dealing strictly with the musical numbers, improvise the lyrics or speak the lyrics as though they were a speech in the script.

Ground Plan. The ground plan is a layout of the setting, a two-dimensional drawing of all objects that break up the stage space: doors, steps, and walls as well as furniture. A creative, well-designed ground plan provides the director and the actors with opportunities to create interesting and productive compositions or arrangements of actors in the setting. These compositions should make visually explicit the dramatic action and conflict of the musical. The ladder in *The Fantasticks*, for example, serves as a wall to divide the stage into the two neighboring pieces of property. It is a crucial element of the ground plan because it visually establishes the conflict, the division, between the two families.

The director, working with the the ground plan and a detailed knowledge of the musical as a result of script and character analysis, is able to create challenging improvisational situations that will permit actors to discover, develop, and demonstrate characterization and action. Use of props and set pieces, to aid in the generation of composition and movement, will further the production of a creative visual design.

When this visual pattern is developed improvisationally and grows naturally from the script and character action, it is known as *organic blocking*. This, then, is the core of working rehearsals. Many of these exercises may be applied to songs as well as to dialogue. It is pointless to have actors develop a clear character relationship in one scene only to follow it with a song that is dramatically unclear. Both songs and dances need to be tied to the action of the nonmusical scenes.

Running Rehearsals. When segments of the show have been worked in detail—dances staged and songs learned—it is time to begin to put the pieces of the puzzle together. Running rehearsals permit both actors and director to get a sense of continuity, to see how songs and dances grow from nonmusical segments. Following are some tips on making running rehearsals productive:

- Run segments of the show regularly within the staging and working rehearsals. The more cohesion the rehearsals can provide for the actors, the better.
- Use running rehearsals as the basis for more working rehearsals to spot problem areas that need ''fixing.''
- Avoid running the same material over and over without stopping to make improvements, or monotony may set in.

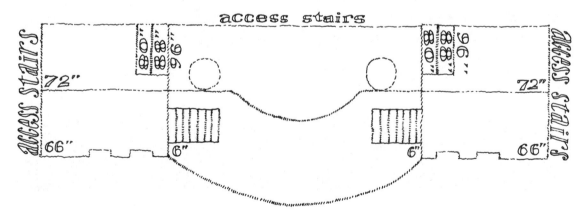

Ground plan for a production of *DAMES AT SEA*, Act II. Note the presence of various levels and stairs to provide interesting use of space with regard to composition and movement. The doors stage right and stage left permit entrance into the area beneath the platforms, and the stairs right and left provide access to the upper levels.

• To keep running rehearsals fresh, use improvisational exercises before the run to encourage spontaneity. This is particularly important
when running larger sections of the script,
such as complete acts.

Polishing Rehearsals. They are just that: the time
to polish off the rough edges and turn a stone into
a gem. During these rehearsals, in the final week
before performance, the director fine-tunes every
moment of the show and coordinates technical aspects of the production with the design team. A
final comment: Polishing rehearsals are a kind of

"last chance." Though the production at this stage
is usually well set, it is never too late to correct a
problem or make a last-minute adjustment. No director should be intimidated by time and allow an
obvious mistake to go unattended simply because
the show opens tomorrow or the next day. After
all, the production will continue to grow and change
in performance.

CHOREOGRAPHY

The choreographer functions in a key position
on the musical production team. In conjunction
with the work of the musical director, the choreog-

Large production numbers need careful attention to detail in staging and spacing. In *1776*, for example,
notice how the focus of the scene is directed toward the primary characters down stage center; but also
notice that all other characters are nicely grouped to highlight their individual mood and attitude in the
scene. (From the production of Wabash College. Directed by Lauren K. Woods. Set design by Michael
voss. Costumes designed by Lynne Emmert.)

Choreography is, in simplest terms, a pattern of movement set to music. There should be a clear and obvious rhythm to the movement and all steps should be counted and orchestrated. The basic principle underlying the creation of effective choreography is "the simpler the better." (From the Smith College production of *THE BOY FRIEND*. Directed by Roberta Sklar. Set design by William E. Hatch. Costume design by George M. Carney. Choreography by Nancye Andrews, Jordan Baker, and Hope Wurcack. Dance consulting by Gemze de Lappe.)

rapher's work is what makes a musical a musical. Without song and dance there would be no difference between a musical and any other play. The choreographer must work closely with the director to help establish the concept, style, or primary idea of the production. If the director is serving as choreographer, that collaboration is already complete.

The choreographer in nonprofessional theatre may be a dance or theatre instructor on the faculty of a college or secondary school, a professional hired specifically for the occasion, or a person with little formal training but years of experience in musical theatre. It is also possible that the choreog-

rapher is the director or is someone who has little experience in choreography. It is therefore important to outline basic principles and procedures for the nondancing or first-time choreographer.

Choreography is, in simplest terms, a pattern of movement set to music. It is true that segments of nonmusical plays are often choreographed. For example, complicated fight scenes need to be set so specifically that they appear to be danced; there is a clear and obvious rhythm to the movement, and all steps are counted or orchestrated. The basic principle underlying the creation of effective choreography is this: The simpler, particularly for the novice choreographer and/or dancers, the better.

A dance performed beautifully and well integrated into the production is a better choice than a splashy production number of mediocre quality. With this principle in mind, let us proceed to the ''why'' of musical theatre choreography.

The presence of song and dance in a musical production, as suggested earlier, creates a heightened form of drama. A character's emotional expression can find an appropriate outlet only in the musical energy of a song or a dance. In *The Fantasticks*, Matt and Luisa's romance inspires them to burst into ''They Were You''; Tony, Maria, Anita, and the two gangs of *West Side Story* are so excited about the evening's prospects that they respond with ''Tonight''; Ruby, the heroine of *Dames at Sea*, is so overcome by the supposed loss of Dick that she sadly sings ''Raining in My Heart.''

Choreography, besides being an outlet for heightened emotion, is also closely tied to the script. Most choreography tells a story and, in doing so, contributes to the unfolding of dramatic action. Musical numbers, particularly in contemporary musical theatre, generally have as much to say as the script or nonmusical segments. (At least the choreographer needs to approach them that way.) Well-planned and well-executed choreography also supports and contributes to the style and the concept of the production and communicates much information about characters.

Thus, there are several legitimate reasons for choreography:

- to serve as a form of heightened emotional expression
- to tell a story or further the action of the show
- to contribute to the style or concept of the show
- to reveal valuable character information.

Some musicals, now somewhat dated, include dances used to spotlight the talents of a particular person, usually a well-known star. Though pleasing to the audience of its day, this type of choreography demands a more legitimate reason for its inclusion in a modern musical. All good choreography serves to entertain the audience, to stimulate its imagination, and to keep its attention riveted on the stage. Choreography entertains best when it is clearly tied to the action of the script.

Planning the Choreography

Long before the actual choreography is taught to the dancers, the choreographer must do his or her homework in preparation for the dance rehearsals. Early meetings with the production staff are important for a number of reasons:

- With the *director*—to get a feeling for the goals of the production and to understand the concept underlying the director's approach to the musical so that the choreography maintains the spirit of the show: the gentle romance of *The Fantasticks*, the 1930s decadence of *Cabaret*, the street-wise toughness of *West Side Story*.
- With the *musical director*—to study the orchestration so that dance patterns and steps conform to the music as to the ''color'' of the orchestration: piano versus brass or reeds.
- With the *scene designer*—to obtain a good sense of the ground plan and to determine how best to use the space.
- With the *costumer*—to have the choreography complement the costumes and vice versa, rather than having one hinder the other.

In addition, the choreographer needs to have an excellent awareness of the show: a clear understanding of what precedes each dance number and what follows. The choreography needs to grow from previous action and contribute to the events that follow; dramatically speaking, dances must not seem to appear from nowhere. The choreographer should study the characters in the same way the director and the actors do. Only by deciding ''who'' a character is can the choreographer determine how, when, why, and where that character moves. Finally, the choreographer may need to research the period of the show. The time and place of the script often determine the style of the choreography. Consider the potential differences in style resulting from the location and storyline of the script when the time is held constant:

Turn-of-the-Century
Oklahoma!—American Midwest
Hello, Dolly—New York City
A Little Night Music—Sweden
Fiddler on the Roof—Russia

1912:
The Music Man—Iowa
My Fair Lady—London

1920s:
Zorba—Greece
The Boy Friend—French Riviera

1930s:
Dames at Sea—New York City
Cabaret—Germany
The Sound of Music—Austria

Some musicals, of course, such as *Cats, The Roar of the Greasepaint, The Smell of the Crowd,* and *Stop the World, I Want to Get Off,* are nonperiod in style and have a universality of time and location.

PERPARING THE CHOREOGRAPHY

Cutting. In the planning stages, the choreographer should settle the matter of cutting dances or parts of dances from the show. This decision is usually made in conjunction with the director and the musical director. Dance numbers that are too complicated or too difficult given the abilities of the cast may be shortened or cut altogether. Dances that serve only to spotlight star performers and contribute little to the dramatic flow of the musical may be eliminated in favor of a tighter, more coherent production. It is not unheard of for a choreographer to cut dances after rehearsals have begun. The assumed or supposed abilities of dancers may fail to materialize. As suggested earlier, simple, shorter dances done well are much more attractive than lengthy, awkward numbers.

The Process. When the choreographer has researched the style of the show, he or she needs to visualize patterns of movement for individual dances based on a study of the play and the characters doing the dancing. Visualizing these patterns necessarily involves the use of the ground plan. The choreographer should work with the director and the scene designer in the planning stages to determine how the setting may be used most effectively. This give-and-take with the production staff may result in design changes that will positively affect both the setting and the choreography. While open expanses of space are necessary for large, active chorus numbers, smaller, more intimate dances may be staged to incorporate step units, platforms, entrances and exits, and furniture. In the same manner, the choreographer needs to consult with the costumer on the effects of costumes on the dancer's freedom of movement.

Patterns of movement are composed of individual steps synchronized to the music. The original cast album of the musical can be very helpful in giving the choreographer a general idea of the music for each number. To insure musical accuracy, however, some songs and dances may have been adjusted for the album; to reinforce the spirit of the orchestration, the choreographer should work with a rehearsal pianist and the actual orchestration.

While some choreography may be stylized movement that is easily taught to dancers, more complicated choreography may demand a detailed teaching process that involves the aid of an assistant choreographer or a competent dance captain. The process may include:

- Breaking the dance down into several sections.
- Demonstrating and teaching difficult steps first, without music.
- Combining series of steps to create patterns of movement.
- Adding music and performing patterns at slower tempos.
- Performing choreography at full tempo.

Individual choreographers have their own system

for writing down choreographic notes. Any type of notation that is practical for the choreographer is useful.

Opening Dance Number. The opening number of the show is crucial. It is the audience's first opportunity to adjust to the style of the production and to become familiar with the characters, setting, and storyline. It is comparable to audience adjustment to the first speech of a character in a nonmusical play. The actor's tone of voice, pitch, volume, and rate—as well as the content of the speech—are quickly absorbed. Always create choreography for the opening number that permits the audience to settle quickly into the world of the show. Some productions have opening songs that aid in this process. For example, in *Dames at Sea*, ''Wall Street'' sets up the location (New York City), the period (1930s), and the personality of one of the leading characters (Mona). ''A Comedy Tonight'' from *A Funny Thing Happened on the Way to the Forum* establishes the spirit of the musical and informs the audience that they are about to be transported to ancient Rome.

Choreography for any musical may be broken down into various combinations of steps, kicks, slides, turns, hops, swings, brushes, crosses, pivots, lifts, leaps, points, and jumps. But, more important, effective choreography accounts for *who* is dancing, *why* they are dancing, *where* they are dancing, and *when* they are dancing. This applies to chorus work as well as to solo and duet numbers. Understanding the who, why, where, and when keeps choreography relevant to the show's style and content and adds mightily to the dramatic action of the script.

WORKING WITH THE PRODUCTION STAFF

As the focal point for all production decisions, the director needs to communicate daily with the other members of the production staff: the musical director, the scene and lighting designers, and the costume designer.

Musical Director. The musical director's contribution to the production team is obvious. After all, this is *musical* theatre. A good musical director can spell the difference between a true stage success and an awkward effort. Coordinating the musical elements of the show is a fearsome task and demands the utmost in talent and commitment. The first job is to locate a skilled, musical director. This person might be on the faculty of a college or high school or a professional musician who free-lances when the time and money are right. As in the case of the choreographer, the musical director might also be an amateur musician who has wide experience serving in this capacity for community groups and organizations.

Regardless of the musical director's professional status or background, he or she must handle several areas of responsibility. The musical director learns the score so that he or she is conversant with the technical difficulties of the vocal score and the orchestration. During auditions, the musical director provides important input regarding the singing capabilities of potential cast members relative to the vocal demands of the show. The musical director also discusses with the director the number of singers necessary to carry the vocal score; some shows require three- or four-part (or more) harmony whereas others use choruses that sing primarily in unison.

During rehearsals, the musical director's duties fall into two broad categories: vocal work with the principals and the chorus, and work with the orchestra. A rehearsal pianist may serve as an assistant musical director by coaching singers and accompanying rehearsals.

Vocal coaching involves teaching musical parts to the entire cast and then rehearsing them constantly to insure their growth as singer/actors, particularly when they begin to dance as well.

The musical director may find it necessary to make adjustments in the score for the singers or the musicians. Transposing music is sometimes necessary, since nonprofessionals are often unable to match the vocal or instrumental range for which the music was composed. It may also be necessary

Patterns of movement are composed of individual steps synchronized to the counts of the music. While some choreography may be stylized movement, like that found in *THE MIKADO*, more complicated choreography may demand a detailed teaching process that involves the aid of an assistant choreographer or a competent dance captain. (From the production of the University of Florida. Directed by Joe Conger. Set design by Dennis Maulden. Costume design by Gweneth West.)

to reduce the orchestration. Though a twenty- or thirty-piece orchestra is ideal, the available musical talent could suggest that a piano, bass, and drums combination is more practical. Such decisions should be made in conjunction with the director and the choreographer, since reductions or adjustments in music will affect the entire production.

The musical director rehearses with the orchestra alone before it joins the cast. The better equipped the orchestra is to deal with the music, the smoother will be the transition to the working rehearsals when director, musical director, and choreographer make changes, however slight. A possible rehearsal schedule for the orchestra might be as follows:

1. Musical director works with the orchestra two to three weeks before the orchestra meets the cast.
2. A week to ten days before the show opens, the orchestra joins the cast for several working rehearsals to set tempos, balance voices with instruments, and maintain the style of the show.
3. Following technical rehearsal (several days before opening) the orchestra has complete runthroughs with the cast; any problems are handled before the next rehearsal.

Collaboration here is crucial. The musical director needs to maintain constant contact with the director, the choreographer, and the designers not only to help insure a consistent style and spirit for the show, but also to work out such technical matters as singers' and dancers' cues, musical bridges, and set changes.

Designers—Scene, Lighting, Costume. The design of scenery, lights, and costumes for musical theatre has evolved over the past few decades. Thirty or forty years ago multiple realistic settings and act-curtains or travelers to cover scene changes were popular. Today, many musicals dating from the 1940s to the 1960s are still produced with traditional, though often mechanized, scenery: wagons moving on a tracked stage, units flown in from above or projected out from wings. It is not uncommon, however, to see shows produced with simplified single or abstract settings. Similarly, advanced technology and equipment permit lighting designers to create dazzling displays of light and shadow. Costume designers adjust their uses of color, fabric, and other materials to keep pace with the changes in scene and lighting design.

The information necessary for these artists to create their designs is obtained from a variety of sources:

- Study of the script and its given circumstances.
- Study of the music for mood and style values.
- Period research based on the given circumstances of the script.
- Discussions with the director regarding concept or approach to the musical.
- Discussions with the choreographer regarding dancers' use of available space.

Ideally, thoughts and feelings about the show, its setting, and its characters are filtered through the designers' imaginations, and the results are designs that coincide with the style set by the director and complement the work of the actors. Discussions among the members of the design staff regarding color, mood, style, and period generate a creative effort whereby sets, lights, and costumes complement each other as well.

There are always practical considerations for each of these designers to confront:

- Costumes must be comfortable and usable for the actors as well as artistically sound.
- The scene designer may have a stringent budget that demands an unusual approach such as abstract or "suggested" settings.
- The lighting designer may not have the most advanced equipment available (in quality or quantity) so ingenuity in its use must make up for lack of materials.

The importance of creative design work to reinforce the production concept must not be underesti-

It is not uncommon to see musicals produced today with simplified, single, or abstract settings. In *LITTLE MARY SUNSHINE*, for example, the production designers adjusted their uses of color, scene painting, and construction to suggest the ''period'' and the ''given circumstances'' of the musical. (From the Stetson University production. Directed by designed by Walter Sonnenburg.)

mated. However, the director bears final responsibility for all that appears on the stage. With that in mind, it is wise, whenever possible, to avoid scenery or lighting effects that call more attention to themselves than to the action on the stage, and scene changes that take too long. Simplicity will solve both of those problems.

Communicating with the Actors

The director's ability to communicate with the actors has a direct impact on the outcome of the show. It is a popular notion in some theatrical circles that the director ''directs,'' often in the style of a drill sergeant: manipulating actors physically, giving orders, providing line readings, and generally telling actors what to do and where to go.

Some sections of any rehearsal process do demand an authoritarian approach: teaching choreography, for example. Very specific feedback from the director may be necessary when an actor is ''lost'' and cannot seem to find the way back to the show. Occasionally, the director needs to lecture in establishing rehearsal goals or to provide research or background information for the benefit of the actors.

However, the nature of the artistic process requires that actors have a certain amount of freedom to provide creative solutions to rehearsal problems: freedom from a director's criticizing, correcting, and lecturing before the actor has had time to experiment, discover, and develop. The director can encourage actors' inventiveness by supporting the discovery process, praising efforts to take risks rather than pursue the tried-and-true, asking questions, and accepting and eliciting ideas from the cast. The improvisational approach to rehearsal described earlier requires this type of directorial behavior. Playing a variety of roles, the director serves as the critic and the prodder as well as the supportive democrat and the directive autocrat.

The director will have plenty of time to establish his or her authority and to instill discipline in the cast. Along the way it is wise to allow for the actors' creative needs and to realize that true creativity is the result of director/actor collaboration.

SUMMARY

The director's task in directing musical theatre sometimes seems overwhelming; indeed, the sheer number of problems and considerations is enough to scare off the most courageous director. Nevertheless, directing a musical is not an impossible task. The job is made less difficult when the director does his or her homework, communicates frequently and thoroughly with the other members of the production staff, and organizes his or her use of time. Thus this chapter closes on a positive note with a suggested production schedule for use by the director, choreographer, musical director, and design staff in the hope that such preplanning will minimize production problems.

SUGGESTED PRODUCTION SCHEDULE

Preliminary work: Entire production staff reads script, studies music, and researches period and style to get a feel for the musical. Director completes script and character analyses and plans auditions.

Week	Activity
1	Staff meets to discuss director's concept, ideas, style of show.
2	Designers present ideas, to which director responds. Choreographer discusses choreography with director and musical director. Cuts and changes in score are discussed. Rehearsal pianist makes tape for choreographer to use during some rehearsals.
3	Show is cast. Designers present sketches for director's feedback and/or approval.
4	Rehearsals begin. Final sketches, ground plan, and costume plot are approved by director. Musical director begins vocal work and choreographer begins teaching choreography. Orchestra members receive parts to learn.
5	Rehearsals, vocal work, choreography continue. Musical director begins work with orchestra. Costume fittings are held, and discussions continue with design staff.
6 & 7	Work of fifth week is continued and refined.

8   Cast begins working on the set. Orchestra joins cast for working rehearsals. Director runs polishing rehearsals.

9   Set is completed, lights and costumes are used for technical and dress rehearsals. Orchestra doing runthroughs with the cast.

10   Show opens.

(Time may be collapsed by combining activities and working at a faster pace. Preliminary work may begin anywhere from 2 weeks to 3 or more months before the production staff first meets.)

Part IV

PRODUCING
THE MUSICAL

PRODUCING THE MUSICAL

The word *produce* suggests "yielding," "creating," or "generating" results. The producer of any theatrical event, including the musical, does just that—gets results! The producer is often the person who initiates the production and the one most responsible for guaranteeing that on opening night a show is presented as promised.

In the professional theatre, the producer must find financial backing for the production. He or she may choose the show being produced, hire the managerial, artistic, and technical staff, and assist in casting. He or she may have generated the concept for the script and assisted the playwright in writing and revising the script. In short, the producer assumes total responsibility for all areas of the production.

In the nonprofessional theatre, particularly institutional or academic theatre, the producer is seldom responsible for obtaining all of the financing necessary for the show. The producer may have input regarding the choice of musical, but given the nature of nonprofessional theatres, rarely does this person hire staff members. Since most musicals done today are revivals of successful shows, the producer seldom assists the playwright in preparing the script for production.

Nevertheless, many similarities exist between the professional and the nonprofessional producer. Both must oversee the financial and business concerns of the musical and facilitate the work of the production staff.

Producing theatre is an awesome, demanding, sometimes exhausting job, but one that is ultimately rewarding when the musical opens and the efforts of many talented and creative people have been coordinated in an exciting fashion. The producer of any type of theatre is often the "unsung hero" of the show. Though not directly responsible for the acting, directing, or design elements of the production, the producer is the "oil" that makes the theatrical machine hum. Without a skillful, organized, creative producer, even the best efforts of the artistic team may go unappreciated.

THE PRODUCER: WEARING SEVERAL HATS

In the nonprofessional theatre the work of the producer may be undertaken by one person or shared by a group of people. Though no one need be designated "producer," the tasks of managing the show from the business point of view must be undertaken by someone. Sometimes the director of the musical in an educational situation also produces the show with the assistance of qualified students and volunteers. Rarely do secondary school theatres hire someone specifically for this purpose. Some colleges, universities, and community theatres, however, are able to supply a person for this post. In the college setting, the producer may also be a member of the regular faculty.

Regardless of how a theatre organization titles its staff or divides the work load, a certain number of managerial and business tasks must be done by someone during the course of the production process. The person responsibile for overseeing these areas, whether called "producer" or not, is indeed the producer of the show. Keep in mind that the professional producer hires separate persons to oversee each of the following areas, whereas the nonprofessional producer often assumes personal responsibility for each one:

1. Budget and purchasing. The day-to-day fiscal operation of the production.
2. Box office. Ticket sales and all box-office business.
3. Subscription sales. If the theatre has a season of shows, mailing of the season brochure and

sale of all season tickets before the opening of the season.

4. Publicity. Promotion and advertising for the production.
5. Group sales. Locating and selling potential group audiences for the production.
6. Front of house. Maintenance of the audience areas of the theatre during performance time.

The nonprofessional producer's work is enormously complicated if he or she serves in an artistic capacity as director or designer of the musical as well. Beyond the day-to-day management of the production, the producer also keeps in close contact with the artistic personnel to assure a smooth working process: making sure that the director has available rehearsal space and sufficient rehearsal time; obtaining the necessary materials and supplies for the designers so that they may complete their work on time; facilitating communication among all members of the production staff by production meetings.

The wise and organized producer establishes a business production schedule similar to that created by the artistic production team, including dates by which all tasks need to be completed. In a complicated musical, such a record-keeping device proves invaluable for the busy producer.

BUDGET AND PURCHASING

Establishing the Budget

The quantity of work to be done by the producer may be determined, in part, by the budget. The amount of money available for the production tells the producer how much can be spent on sets, costumes, and lights as well as on advertising, promotion, and general audience development. In addition, the size of the budget may determine the choice of show. Large-cast musicals with several sets may not be affordable for the modest theatre company that is producing its first musical. Multiple costume and set changes are expensive. Compare the cost of producing *Oklahoma!* with that of

The Fantasticks. Royalties and rental of show materials from the rental agency may also dictate show selection. Some musicals cost hundreds of dollars more than others, depending on number of performances and size of theatre.

The producer cannot create a production budget until he or she knows exactly how much money is available. Many educational theatres are subsidized by institutional funding; some community theatres have a comfortable financial cushion established over time; others must break even and count on ticket sales to support the entire show. Whatever the source of financial support, the producer must assess the theatrical organization realistically when creating the budget. For a theatre dependent on its box office, it is a little dangerous to assume 100 percent capacity for every performance and thus budget the show to break even based on this ideal attendance figure. On the other hand, it is wise to make conservative estimates of box-office revenue, thus providing a cash overage when the show comes in at or near budget. Regardless of the type of producing agency, emergencies and unforeseen circumstances often force the show to run over the established budget, and the prudent manager allows for such contingencies.

The producer establishes the budget by allocating amounts of money in all areas of potential spending. These may include:

- Costumes.
- Technical areas such as scenery, lighting equipment and supplies, props.
- Promotion and publicity.
- Salaries and stipends for personnel.
- Royalties and rental of materials.
- Expenses incurred during production that do not fall into one of the above categories.

Based on discussions with the director, costumer, and scene and lighting designers regarding the demands of the show, the cost of royalties, and projected publicity and advertising expenses, the producer creates a Projected Show Budget. It must be remembered that this is an *estimate* of expenses. Following the close of the production, the producer

BUSINESS PRODUCTION SCHEDULE

Week	*Activity*
1	Prepare show and season budgets
	Design and print season brochure or brochure for the musical alone
	Order press packages for the season or for the musical alone
	Order tickets
2	Oversee the purchase of materials for sets and costumes
	Distribute musical materials—scores, books, orchestral parts
3	Prepare brochure for mailing
	Design layouts and print graphic materials: posters, placemats, buttons, etc.
4	Issue press release on season
	Prepare mailings to groups, high schools
	Contact reviewers for local newspapers
	Make sure brochure is in the mail
5	Issue press release on the musical itself, announcing the cast
	Design ads and determine location and number of placements
6	Issue press release on the musical itself, including plot summary
	Prepare large signs for placement outside the theatre
	Prepare a marquee for the theatre noting show title and dates
7	Issue individual press releases on cast members
	Shoot and develop publicity pictures
	Print additional flyers or handouts
8	Place ads
	Prepare lobby display
	Mail publicity pictures
	Send program copy to printer
	Distribute posters
9	Release feature story to local newspaper
	Open box office
	Distribute flyers, buttons, or other handouts
10	Take and develop production pictures
	Finalize lobby display
	Show opens

prepares the accounting of actual expenses, noting the difference between projected budget and actual money spent.

Obtaining the Rights to Production

When the musical has been chosen for production, the business manager or producer must obtain permission to perform the show from the agency holding the rights. Most musicals are held by one of several agencies:

- Tams-Witmark
- Samuel French
- Music Theatre International
- Rodgers-Hammerstein Library

(See Appendix for addresses.)

When applying for the rights, the producing organization must provide information on ticket prices, number of seats in the theatre, and number of performances planned. The rental agency should be contacted first, since some have a specific application form that must be submitted. When the agency receives a completed application form, it sends the producer a contract to be signed and returned. The contract specifies the cost of renting the musical materials and the royalty fees for performance. Since the cost of the rights may be a substantial part of the show's budget, information on rights should be obtained well in advance of the production process.

Purchasing

It is likely that the person serving as producer will be responsible for handling all expenses involved in the production. When the budget has been established, the specific outlay of funds must be closely monitored by the producer. Many academic institutions use purchase orders for payment for goods and services. Since this type of payment generally requires patience on the part of the vendor (some purchase orders require weeks to be fully processed), many businesses must approve the use of purchase orders in advance.

The simplest methods of purchasing are:

1. Reimbursing persons for out-of-pocket expenses upon submission of appropriate receipts.
2. Distributing a cash allowance to persons responsible for buying materials and keeping a close watch on outlay by obtaining receipts for all items purchased.
3. Issuing checks for the total cost of purchasing large items or bulk materials.

All of the above assume that the producer has a cash account at his or her disposal. If such money is not available or if the producer only has access to a petty cash account for emergencies, he or she must follow the progress of the purchase orders carefully—from purchasing office to vendor to accounting office—to insure as rapid a payment to the vendor as possible.

The producer can save both time and money when purchasing by buying materials in bulk, since larger quantities are often cheaper than smaller single purchases; by buying materials when on sale or when a special offer is advertised; and by buying supplies and materials year-round if the theatre operates on a seasonal basis with more than one production.

PROJECTED SHOW BUDGET
FOR *THE BOY FRIEND*

Technical	$ 3,000.00
Construction of set/set pieces	
Lighting supplies	
Rental of sound equipment	
Construction and purchase of hand props	
Costumes—construction and rental	$ 1,500.00
Business	$ 2,000.00
Publicity	
Advertising	
Promotional materials and services	
Royalty and rental of musical materials	$ 2,575.00
Rehearsal accompanists	$ 1,700.00
TOTAL	$10,775.00

It is valuable to have the time to shop around and obtain the best bargains when the pressures of producing a single show are not predominant.

Accounting

One of the most important duties of the producer is the creation of a simple, organized system for

(1) TRANSACTION CODE S/C	(2) BATCH NUMBER	(3) NEW/ MATCH	STATE OF NEW JERSEY	(4) FISCAL YEAR	(5) TRANSACTION DATE	(6) DOC TYP	(7) DOCUMENT NUMBER	(8) REJECT INDICATOR
47 0						I		

AGENCY PURCHASE ORDER/INVOICE

VENDOR STATUS

BLANK = NO CHANGE
1 = NEW VENDOR
2 = ADDRESS CHANGE
3 = LOCATION CODE
4 = NEW VENDOR AND LOCATION
5 = VENDOR NO. CORRECTION

(9) ACCOUNT NUMBER				(10)	(11)	(12)				(13)	(14)	(15)	(16)
ORGANIZATION	FUND	PROGRAM	OBJECT	COST CENTER	PROJECT ACTIVITY	EXTENDED NO.				TOTAL AMOUNT	AGENCY P.O. NUMBER	OBLIGATION NUMBER	

VENDOR NAME AND ADDRESS

CONTACT FOR INFORMATION (NAME AND PHONE NO.)

(17) NAME, STREET, CITY, STATE, ZIP CODE

IF DIRECT PURCHASE OR SPECIAL PROCUREMENT, INDICATE DATE QUOTATION RECEIVED

BILL TO: ENTER COMPLETE NAME AND ADDRESS

SHIP TO:

FOLD
MARK

(18) COMMODITY CODE	VENDOR INVOICE NUMBER	(19)	(20) VENDOR IDENTIFICATION NUMBER	CONTRACT NUMBER

INSTRUCTIONS TO VENDOR: (1) YOU MUST USE THE ATTACHED STATE INVOICE FORM (ORIGINAL AND DUPLICATES) FOR BILLING PURPOSES. (2) IF THIS IS A PARTIAL BILLING, YOU MUST SUBMIT BALANCES ON SEPARATE STATE INVOICE FORMS. (3) ENCLOSE PACKING SLIP WITH SHIPMENTS. (4) SHOW OBLIGATION NUMBER AND ACCOUNT NUMBER ON ALL BILLS OF LADING, INVOICES, AND CORRESPONDENCE. (5) ADDRESS ALL CORRESPONDENCE TO THE STATE AGENCY INDICATED ABOVE.

CASH DISCOUNT

ITEM NO.	QUANTITY	UNIT	DELIVER THE FOLLOWING ITEMS F.O.B. DESTINATION DESCRIPTION	UNIT PRICE	AMOUNT

AGENCY APPROVAL: Signature affixed to this purchase order serves as certification: 1) that items purchased under DPA authorization are not currently available under the provisions of a current State contract or from the State distribution center; and 2) that funds required and authorized for this purpose are obligated and available. Unauthorized use subject to prosecution.

TOTAL OBLIGATION AMOUNT

TYPE OF PURCHASE AUTHORIZATION (Check one)
- [ ] ANNUAL CONTRACT AUTHORIZATION
- [ ] BLANKET ORDER
- [ ] DIRECT PURCHASE AUTHORIZATION
- [ ] SPECIAL PROCUREMENT AUTHORIZATION

(AUTHORIZED SIGNATURE)   (TITLE)

(PRINTED OR TYPED NAME OF AUTHORIZING EMPLOYEE)   (DATE)

the accounting of all money spent. This includes keeping a careful record of all receipts and cash outlays; filing receipts systematically for future use; keeping copies of all invoices received; keeping bookkeeping records up-to-date; and making certain that all materials and services are received in appropriate quantities, in good order, and on time.

Though even the most efficient organization has problems occasionally, careful budgeting, purchasing, and accounting practices help keep productivity high.

BOX OFFICE

The producer may also serve as the chief box-office treasurer, handling the income from ticket sales as well as outgoing money. Though there may be a separate overseer of the box office and its procedures, the producer must still maintain watch over ticket revenue. This revenue forms the credit side of the theatre's accounting and helps to balance the debit side.

It is both practical and wise to have as few people as possible responsible for box-office work, since the greater the number of people involved, the greater the margin for error. However, it must be recognized that many academic and community theatres require the use of unskilled volunteers. Thus, a simple system for selling tickets works the best. Close daily monitoring of all box-office personnel helps to eliminate gross errors in the exchange of tickets and money.

Establishing the Box Office

A clean, well-lit, well-organized, secure space forms the basis for a box office. The box office is the "heart" of the business operation of the theatre, and it needs to be kept in good pumping order. There is nothing quite so debilitating as a messy, disorganized place where tickets, ticket orders, cash box, and subscription forms are strewn across a single work table. It is often said that working in a box office is a thankless, tedious, boring job. Nonetheless, it is one of the most crucial jobs in

the theatre, particularly so when that theatre is greatly dependent on ticket revenue for survival.

The theatre box office needs to be located in a place that:

* is easily accessible to potential patrons;
* does not block the flow of traffic into the theatre proper;
* is near the theatre and not too far from the street.

In a well-established theatre, the box office is likely to be a permanent fixture of the lobby, secure, and constructed to handle the maximum number of people in a minimum amount of time.

On the other hand, if the theatre is using an essentially nontheatrical space—a school gymnasium, for example—there may be no actual box office. In such a case, the personnel involved need to create a temporary structure. This may be a portable booth of some sort that creates an atmosphere of "separation" from the customers. If on the nights of performance the only available box office is a folding table in the lobby of the theatre, make the most of this makeshift device. Set up as formal a place as possible: The public may think it is only a card table with a cash box, but you know that it is really a box office!

Most important, the box office must have racks so that tickets may be easily accessible by performance; cash drawers or cash boxes; access to a telephone; and ample work space. In addition, it may be helpful to have office equipment within easy reach: typewriter, calculator, stationery.

TICKETS

There are various ways of handling tickets. Since the ticket represents an agreement between the theatrical organization and the patron regarding the latter's right to a seat, each ticket represents an actual or potential exchange of money and should be treated as such. Few theatres operate without the use of some sort of ticket. Some Off-Off-Broadway theatres, for example, simply check the names of audience members off a Reservation List as they enter the theatre. But, generally, patrons expect a ticket and theatres usually oblige.

A theatre may choose among several types of tickets, depending on certain considerations:

- The budget of the show. Printed tickets are more expensive than computer tickets or tickets that are partially filled in by theatre personnel.
- The size of the theatre. A small theatre may choose not to have reserved seating, so that all tickets permit audience members to sit wherever they choose.
- The permanence of the theatre space. If the theatre is only temporary, chances are that the seats are temporary as well and not numbered, dictating a general-admission policy.
- The formality of the organization. Some community or school theatres that are operating on a shoestring budget and producing their first musical may choose to photocopy small pieces of paper as tickets and fill in seat information by hand.

Types of Tickets. There are ticket types to suit every form of theatre, from the most sophisticated and professional-looking to the simplest and cheapest. Before deciding upon type, the producer should obtain cost estimates from a variety of sources. Generally, the producer will choose one of the following:

Printed tickets supplied by a ticket company. They are still used by some Broadway theatres, although most now use a computer-generated ticket.
- Computer ticket supplied by a company and looking like a computer printout.
- Ticket partially printed or duplicated, with seat location filled in by the theatre.

The tickets may also be printed, at greater expense, with a detachable audit stub that may be used in box-office accounting: The stub is removed if the ticket is sold at a reduced or discounted rate.

When ordering tickets, the theatre needs to supply all necessary information, usually in writing, so that there can be no mistake in printing. That information includes the name of the theatrical organization, the location of the theatre, the show title, day, date, and time of performance, and the ticket price. Many theatres simply print the standard price on the face of the ticket, and if the ticket is sold at a discount it is so stamped on the reverse. If tickets are for reserved seating, a copy of the theatre's seating chart must be included with the print order. If the seats are general admission, they may be numbered consecutively.

Selling the Tickets. It is important for the box office to establish a simple, effective system for selling tickets. The ticket-selling procedure ought to be viewed as another opportunity to promote the theatrical organization as well as the show. From the moment the patron walks to the box-office window or dials the phone to make a reservation, the best foot of the theatre should be put forward.

Before tickets are made available to the general public, the producer removes *house seats*: complimentary tickets for newspaper reviewers, tickets for visiting VIPs, or tickets to be used in case of a problem or emergency, or at the discretion of the producer. House seats are usually good seats in the orchestra; sometimes it is wise to hold tickets that are also easily accessible in the event that they are used for the handicapped or for latecomers.

Tickets should be racked or otherwise displayed to the staff well in advance of the opening of the box office. If the theatre is a community or school organization, the box office is probably open for a limited time before the opening of the musical. Box-office staff unfamiliar with the theatre should use seating charts.

Following are some principles for consideration when establishing box-office policies:

1. Set box-office hours and keep them! The public will accommodate itself to whatever time period is established, as long as it is reliable. Using a phone tape when the box office is closed will keep customer complaints to a minimum.

MEMORIAL AUDITORIUM

2. Teach the staff to be courteous but firm with the public, offering the best seats available without unduly prolonging the ticket transaction.

3. For phone reservations, be sure to obtain the correct information: name and initial, date and day of requested tickets, number and type (if discounted) of tickets involved, phone number. All information should be repeated for accuracy, and the patron should be told when to pick up the tickets and what is the total due.

4. When handling window sales, the staff must be careful to select correct tickets, mark off the sale record accurately, note the seat locations on the seating chart to keep ticket availability up-to-date, stamp or otherwise indicate discounted tickets, and give the patron the correct change.

5. As the sale of tickets proceeds, the box-office staff should "dress the house," that is, seat patrons in the best seats first, seating from the center outwards and, at the same time, balancing all areas of the house. If attendance is limited, this practice will suggest that a larger number of people are present than actually are.

6. Keep an accurate record of all sales, both on an hourly and on a daily basis, noting day of sale, number of tickets, date of performance for which the tickets are sold, seat location, type of ticket, and whether standard or discounted.

7. When the show closes, the producer should

SALE RECORD FORM

Date_____

Total $ at open _____
Total $ at close _____

Initials of Cashier	Date of Performance	No. of Tickets and Location	Unit Price	Total

make a final audit of the box office to reconcile total tickets sold with total revenue.

Maintaining a smooth-running box office can be a difficult and time-consuming job. Nevertheless, orderliness, accuracy, and efficiency will pay off, literally, for the producing organization.

PUBLICITY

The producer may also be serving as "publicist," or director of promotional materials for the musical. The very existence of the theatre organization depends on the degree to which the public is made aware of both the theatre and the show. A musical offers ample opportunities for the producer to "get the word out."

The objective of all theatre publicity is, obviously, to attract an audience. Hopefully, these patrons will enjoy the musical and want to return for future productions. Good publicity not only serves the present but helps to create a future for the producing organization. The energetic, innovative publicist uses time and many interesting approaches to the musical to find different ways of saying the same thing: Come See Our Show!

Mailings

The mailing list is the producer's best friend. Sending a specific piece of information (a flyer or brochure) to a specific individual is the surest way of reaching a wide potential audience. Since most theatres use a mailing system that permits them to use a bulk mailing rate, the cost per item mailed is much less than first class. Mailing thousands of brochures will still be somewhat costly, but the return on this type of investment is worth the expense.

Creating and Maintaining a Mailing List. The primary task facing the producer is the compilation of names for a mailing list. They may be derived from a variety of sources: persons who have been to the theatre, reserved tickets, requested information, or attended events similar to the one you are promoting. When people call the theatre requesting information on a particular show, they should be added to the mailing list. The same procedure applies to mail orders. There may be a mailing-list form in the program that patrons can fill out and return to the box office. All these known customers should form the basis of the mailing list.

Sources from which the producer might borrow lists to create a permanent mailing list are local arts organizations such as museums, symphony orchestras, and chamber music societies; local arts councils; and civic, charitable, and other nonprofit clubs and organizations. Some companies specialize in selling lists for theatre use, but these can be expensive and outside the budget of the average academic or community theatre.

Once a mailing list has been created, it is crucial to keep it up-to-date, adding new names, deleting names where appropriate, and changing addresses when patrons move. Mailing lists may be stored in a computer file. This is particularly convenient if the theatre is on a college campus where a computer center can generate labels for mailing purposes. If the budget permits, there are mailing houses that specialize in the maintenance of lists, the labeling of materials, and the preparation of the mailing for the post office. If you are handling the mailing without the aid of a professional organization, it is wise to check with the post office to determine procedures. If bulk mailings are marked "Return requested," deletions and changes in the list can be made easily.

Mailer. If the theatre is operating a season of productions, it pays to create a brochure that advertises the season as a whole, thus usually permitting a subscription service. The advantages of a subscribed season are obvious:

1. Patrons who subscribe to a season of plays create a core of committed audience members. Often they are willing to buy tickets without knowing every show to be presented.
2. Season publicity reduces the amount of publicity required for individual productions.
3. A subscription service is an excellent way to handle a season of plays that has a variety of

popular appeal. One or two extremely popular productions, such as a musical, may sell an entire season that contains new works or experimental plays.

Press Release

A series of well-timed press releases is the cheapest and most effective way, after mailings, of reaching large numbers of people. The press release is, essentially, a news story on the musical or some aspect of the musical. As such it should adhere to the basic standards of newswriting, giving the *who, where, when, what, why,* and *how* of the event. Like a news story, the most important information is given in the first paragraph; thus, if the release has to be shortened the editor can delete by paragraphs.

A series of press releases, each focusing on one aspect of the musical, may be written and released in a time frame that allows maximum coverage. Consider the following:

- 7 weeks before opening, a press release announcing the season as a whole and promoting season subscription.
- 6 weeks before opening, a press release announcing the cast for the first show, the musical.
- 5 weeks before opening, a press release providing background information on the show and listing ticket sale information.
- 3 weeks before opening, press releases on members of the cast.
- 2 weeks before opening, a press release on the director or other prominent member of the production staff, cast, or crew.

The musical itself might suggest additional opportunities for news releases. It is important to adhere to the style of the standard news article when writing the release. Information provided should be factual and straightforward. Adjectives, particularly hackneyed ones such as ''hilarious'' and ''sensational,'' should be kept to a minimum. Nonetheless, press releases need to be interestingly written with short, crisp sentences, accurate spelling of all names, and correct dates. It is wise to provide sufficient information in the release. For example, describing the plot of the musical is a good idea; knowing what the show is about is often a selling point for patrons.

The format of the press release is as follows: It is double-spaced on one side of the paper, with the theatre, address, press contact, telephone number, and release date or FOR IMMEDIATE RELEASE clearly indicated. At the bottom of the first page, if followed by succeeding pages, type MORE in the lower right-hand corner. Number each page in the upper right-hand corner beginning with the second page, and close each press release with END or the symbols ###.

The press release is one of the primary tools of the producer and costs the theatre very little. Because it is newsworthy information and newspapers are in the news business, it will be printed. Many newspapers have arts and entertainment pages established solely for the type of press release you are sending.

Feature Story. In addition to the standard press release, the producer may also write a feature story. This is an article that focuses on one particular aspect of the musical and is sent to a single newspaper, often for publication in a weekend feature section. It may be written from the point of view of the director, playwright, or producer, or it may be an interview with one of them discussing the work involved in doing the musical or describing problems encountered. Good publicity photographs enhance the value of the feature story.

For the novice producer or publicist attempting to create the show's publicity alone or with little help, ready-made press packages may serve as the basis for press releases and specialty stories. Package Publicity Service is a company that provides press packages on most musicals at a very nominal fee. The package contains a history of the show, a list of original cast members and casts of subsequent revivals in New York, a variety of reviews, sample releases and ideas for feature stories, and sample

PRESS RELEASE

September 20, 1985

FOR IMMEDIATE RELEASE
FOR FURTHER INFORMATION: CALL SUZANNE TRAUTH (201) 893-4205

THE BOY FRIEND OPENS SEASON

THE BOY FRIEND, Sandy Wilson's 1920's musical spoof, opens the Montclair State College Major Theatre Series' 1985-86 season.

This musical comedy depicts the Jazz Age in all its glory, from the flappers and the Charleston to the charming romances of young girls and boys. The Major Theatre Series' production of THE BOY FRIEND runs for two weekends, Thursday through Saturday, October 17–19 and October 24–26 at 8:00 p.m. in Memorial Auditorium on the campus of Montclair State College, Upper Montclair, New Jersey. There will be a matinee on Friday, October 18, at 2:15 p.m. Ticket prices are: Standard $5, Senior Citizen and MSC Faculty, Staff, and Alumni $4, and Students with ID $2.50. Call (201) 893-4205, 9:00 a.m. to 5:00 p.m. for information on season subscriptions. Starting October 7, call (201) 746-9120, 10:00 a.m. to 7:00 p.m., for ticket reservations.

THE BOY FRIEND tells an enchanting story—Polly, a lonely rich girl, falls in love with Tony, a handsome messenger boy. Although Polly and Tony believe they could be happy with each other in ''A Room in Bloomsbury,'' their romance seems doomed by Tony's low social standing. Fortunately, his true identity is revealed and all turns out well for the young lovers. Polly and Tony's romance is highlighted by the flirtations of young and old alike as they frolic along the French Riviera. Musical highlights include the title song ''The Boy Friend'' and the lively, showstopping ''Won't You Charleston With Me?''

The innocence and the endearing affectations of this lavish age are reproduced through the colorful costumes, the tuneful melodies, and the energetic dance numbers. THE BOY FRIEND is a nostalgic trip to a merry era.

Dee Dee Sandt directs and choreographs the production. Set design is by John Figola, and Ron Gasparinetti has designed the lights. The costumes have been created by Bruce Goodrich, and Ruthann Hyson is the stage manager for the production. The cast includes: Tim Herman (TONY), Linda Bray (POLLY), Stephen W.R. Bienskie (BOBBY), Kimberly Palmisano (MAISIE), Emi-Rae Hartman (DULCIE)), Rachel Bachman (FAY), Kelly Gomez (NANCY), Jennifer Russell (MADAME DUBONNET), Kira M. Sonin (HORTENSE), Mark Lee (PERCIVAL BROWN), Daniel Kahn (LORD BROCKHURST), Ellen Saylor (LADY BROCKHURST), Steve Sizer (MARCEL), Albert Fernandez (PIERRE), Ken Kozikowski (ALPHONSE and THE TANGO DANCER), Mark McCausland (GUY and THE WAITER), Liza Ciminelli (DENISE), and Dawn Ward (LOLITA).

The remainder of the Major Theatre Series includes: THE LARK, December 4–7; EXTREMITIES, March 12–15; the SPRING DANCE FESTIVAL, April 10–12; THE IMAGINARY INVALID, May 7–10.

###

slogans and phrases describing the show. They provide a good supplement to the producer's own creative writing.

Radio and Television Releases. Releases intended to be read on the radio or television should follow the same basic format as those sent to the newspaper, with a few notable exceptions. Television and radio releases should be typed completely in capital letters, be triple-spaced, and indicate reading time at the top of each paragraph of copy: 30, 20, 10 seconds. Again, the first paragraph should contain the primary information, with succeeding paragraphs elaborating on various aspects of the musical.

Advertising

The primary difference between advertising and the forms of publicity already described is cost. While press releases cost the theatre nothing but mailing expenses, paid advertising can be very expensive, particularly in daily newspapers with large circulation. Nevertheless, when you purchase space you are assured of the ad's placement and content. Press releases are printed at the discretion of the newspaper.

When considering the placement of ads in local newspapers, it is important for the producer to obtain information:

- Ad rates. Most periodicals and newspapers quote rates on a per-line basis. The producer needs to know the number of lines in a column inch of ad space to determine the cost of the ad.
- Deadlines and publication day.
- The section in which the ad will be printed; arts and entertainment sections are best.

A publicity picture. The information on the show, the *cutline*, should be attached to the back of the picture or typed on a sheet of paper that folds over the front. The picture itself should be simple, clear, without extreme contrasts of black and white, and expressive of actor behavior or feeling.

- Circulation of the paper. The greater the number of readers, the higher the cost of advertising.
- Type of copy. To what degree will the use of art and photographs increase the cost?

To insure accuracy in advertising, request a proof of each ad before it is printed.

Paid ads should contain, at a minimum, the information necessary for a potential customer to make a reservation or purchase a ticket: name of the theatre, address, telephone number, schedule of performances (dates and times), play title, author, and ticket price. If the budget permits additional space, a blurb on the show, a phrase or slogan, or a graphic are good attention-getting devices. The producer should design the ad or approve the design if it is created by someone else or an outside agency. Never leave the design up to the newspaper's composing room! Indicate exactly how you want the ad laid out. Whatever the design, the ad needs to attract and hold the attention of people unfamiliar with the show and the theatre until they can absorb the information contained in it. The budget for the musical determines the extent of advertising. Be sure to get your money's worth! Avoid crowding the ad. Some white space and an attractive border serve to set off the copy.

Playbill

Programs or playbills that are distributed in the theatre also serve as a form of publicity. The primary purpose of the program is to assist the audience members in identifiying the performers, characters, action, and setting of the play, as well as the time frame. Many playbills also contain material that publicizes the remainder of the season or other activities of the theatrical organization. The program contains a title page giving the name of the theatre, the producing organization, dates of performance, and the title and authors of the musical. It also gives the cast of characters in order of appearance, the setting time and place, names of members of the artistic staff (director, choreographer, design-

ers, musical director), a statement indicating the permission of the rental agency to produce the show, and acknowledgments of the loan of materials or provision of production assistance. Depending on the length of the playbill, the producer may also want to include the production staff (construction crews, wardrobe and lighting personnel, front-of-house staff), house rules regarding smoking, eating, drinking, and picture-taking in the theatre, and a listing of upcoming events if the theatre runs a seasonal operation.

Many programs include production notes on the show or a note from the director regarding the current production. Brief biographies of the artistic staff and the cast may also be given. Some theatres, nonprofessional as well as professional, sell advertising that pays for the playbill and enables them to enlarge the program to include the ads and additional copy. Such ad selling is a time-consuming activity, and the producer needs to decide whether the benefits will equal the effort. If personnel are available, particularly in the case of a community theatre where volunteer help is plentiful, it is a good idea to pursue advertising to pay for playbills and perhaps to cover other expenses as well.

Finally, the producer should control the format and layout of the program. Whether it is typeset on expensive paper or typed by the theatre staff and duplicated on inexpensive paper, the general design and layout should reflect the musical. It is wise to obtain estimates for the cost of printing well in advance. Several factors, such as outsize programs, the use of graphics and photographs, and glossy paper, will affect the total cost of the playbill.

Graphic Publicity

Graphic materials that are attractive, eye-catching, and well displayed in the community are a valuable source of publicity. The most popular example is the poster. There is much disagreement among publicists on the effectiveness of posters. Yet it cannot be denied that, if well placed, posters can reach nearly as many people as advertising in

Imagination in the publicity of the musical production includes an interesting approach to advertising. Here is an excellent example of how a production number could be used to advertise the musical in local newspapers. (From the production of the University of Minnesota's Centennial Showboat musical *THE BELL OF NEW YORK*. Directed and choreographed by Robert Moulton. Scenery, props, costumes, and lighting design by Janet M. Ryger.)

the local newspaper. Both professional and non-professional theatres make consistent use of posters, and their effectiveness increases when they are reinforced by mailings, ads, and press releases.

Generally, posters are large enough to be seen quickly by passersby. Like the ad, the poster reflects the musical and makes a statement about it to attract people. A good poster should sell a ticket on the spot! Minimal information is similar to that of the ad: name and location of the theatre, phone number, title and authors of the musical, dates and times, and ticket prices. However, the overall effect needs to be greater than the sum of its parts—the poster should suggest that the musical is "a fun evening of theatre," "a startling experience," or "a mysterious adventure."

Since the poster is a graphic form of publicity,

design and color are crucial. It is wise to obtain the services of a graphic artist when putting the poster together. The producer will, of course, determine how much can be spent on the poster. Size, weight of paper stock, color of paper, number of colors used in printing, and printing specialties such as reverses and screening of colors will affect overall cost.

A danger in the design of posters is making them works of art that do little to sell the show. It is important to call attention to the musical and not to the poster itself.

Place posters carefully to cover the largest area possible, emphasizing the locations that are most likely to provide potential customers. Vendors are more likely to display an attractive poster than a plain one, and more likely to do so if offered a pair

Effective poster design includes a sharp simple graphic that reflects the mood of the show.

of complimentary tickets, provided the theatre can afford to do so.

Reduced copies of the poster may be used as handouts to be distributed in areas adjacent to the theatre. The poster design may also be used for the cover of the playbill.

Gimmicks. In addition to posters and flyers, the theatre may generate publicity through the use of other graphic materials. Printed placemats may be distributed at restaurants or, in the case of school productions, in cafeterias. Balloons, buttons, or bumper stickers imprinted with the logo of the show may be distributed. Finally, the loby of the theatre is an ideal location for graphic publicity. Photo-

graphs or head shots of the cast, material on the musical itself or the period in which it occurs, and signs announcing upcoming activities are all effective ways of promoting the theatre and the show.

The most effective publicity is that which is repeated regularly and well timed: The mailing is reinforced by the press releases, which are reinforced by the paid ads, the posters, other graphic materials, and the lobby display. Publicity is simply taking various approaches to obtain the same objective: sale of tickets! Once a show has opened, it is helpful to determine the strength of the publicity campaign. Audience surveys are popular ways of checking on the effectiveness of various forms of publicity.

AUDIENCE SURVEY FORM

PLEASE HELP US SERVE YOU MORE EFFECTIVELY! WE WOULD APPRECIATE YOUR FILLING OUT THIS QUESTIONNAIRE AND PLACING IT IN THE BOX IN THE LOBBY BEFORE YOU LEAVE THE THEATRE. THANK YOU.

1. SUBSCRIBER: YES __ NO__
2. ZIP CODE: _____
3. AGE: UNDER 18 __ 18–25 __ 26–39 __ 40–50 __ 51–65 __ OVER 65 __
4. MSC FACULTY/STAFF __ MSC STUDENT __ MSC ALUMNI __
5. EDUCATION: HIGH SCHOOL __ HIGH SCHOOL GRADUATE __
                     SOME COLLEGE __
                     CURRENTLY ENROLLED IN COLLEGE __
                     UNDERGRADUATE DEGREE __
                     GRADUATE DEGREE __
6. HOW DID YOU HEAR ABOUT THIS SHOW?
    MAILING PIECE __
    NEWSPAPER ADVERTISING __
    POSTER/FLYER __
    FRIEND __
    OTHER _____
7. HOW MANY MAJOR THEATRE SERIES' PRODUCTIONS HAVE YOU SEEN THIS SEASON?
    5 __ 4 __ 3 __ 2 __ 1 __
8. ARE YOU ON OUR MAILING LIST? YES __ NO __
    (IF NOT, AND YOU WISH TO BE, PLACE NAME AND ADDRESS ON REVERSE SIDE OF THIS SHEET.)

THANK YOU.

Group Sales

Letters sent directly to groups and organizations serve as an additional form of mailing that will bolster attendance at the musical. Churches, civic organizations, other theatres, men's and women's clubs, and other high schools and colleges are ex-cellent targets for group sales efforts. A list of potential groups can be created by consulting phone books in area counties, checking with the local Chamber of Commerce, and obtaining lists of schools and colleges in the area. Over a period of time it can be determined which of these groups are likely to respond to invitations to the theatre

GROUP LETTER

DATE

Dear Community Leader:

THE MAJOR THEATRE SERIES OF MONTCLAIR STATE COLLEGE HAS A SEASON THAT IS ABOUT TO EXPLODE—WITH THEATRE THAT IS DELIGHTFULLY CHARMING, WONDERFULLY HILARIOUS, AND ENORMOUSLY POWERFUL! You and your group are invited to be a part of our dynamic 1985-1986 festival of exciting, dramatic events.

We are proud to open our season with THE BOY FRIEND, a musical valentine to the innocence and high spirits of the JAZZ AGE. You and your group will relive the days of the Charleston, flappers, short skirts, and bobbed hair. Romance and hilarity abound when the girl friends meet the boy friends in this toe-tapping, tuneful, witty spoof on the roaring twenties.

This entertaining production is a musical extravaganza that will provide an enjoyable evening of fun-packed nostalgia for the members of your organization. THE BOY FRIEND is singing and dancing merriment at its finest!

We'd like to invite you and your group to take advantage of a terrific bargain. General admission tickets are $5.00, but our special group rate for groups of 15 or more is a remarkable $3.00. Members of your organization can donate the money they save to your group's treasury. A great way to do a little fundraising.

The Major Theatre Series production of THE BOY FRIEND will be presented in Memorial Auditorium and will run two weekends, Thursday through Saturday: October 17–19, October 24–26 at 8:00 p.m. There is a Friday matinee on October 18 at 2:15 p.m.

If you and your group would like to attend a performance of THE BOY FRIEND, please contact us before October 11 for reservations. For additional information, please call 893-4205 between 9:00 a.m. and 5:00 p.m., Monday through Friday. Enclosed please find a season brochure listing future productions. Why not plan to attend a later show as well? We look forward to hearing from you.

Thank you in advance for your interest.

Sincerely,

Dr. Suzanne Trauth
Managing Director, Major Theatre Series

and which are not and thus can be eliminated. A group letter should describe the advantages of the group such as the reduced cost of tickets and the use of the theatre tickets as a form of fund-raising for the group.

HOUSE MANAGEMENT

Depending on the number of personnel available for the management of the theatre, the producer may find himself or herself organizing and managing the "front-of-the-house" operation, otherwise known as house management. The house manager is responsible for the control, comfort, and handling of the audience and any problems arising in the areas adjacent to the theatre's lobby or house. The house manager needs to be capable of handling emergencies, of diplomatically controlling difficult customers, and of supervising a staff.

Though the duties attached to this job are more extensive in some professional theatres, even in nonprofessional theatre they are ample to keep the house manager very busy:

1. Supervising the front-of-house staff: ticket takers, ushers, checkroom and concessions personnel. In the institutional theatre, this may also imply finding and organizing the ushers and ticket takers, particularly if the theatre operates on a volunteer basis.
2. Overseeing the physical condition of the theatre and adjacent spaces, checking to see that the house, lobby, and restrooms are clean and notifying the custodial staff when such cleaning is necessary.
3. Handling customer problems such as complaints about seating or the temperature of the theatre.
4. Coordinating curtain times with the stage manager and notifying the audience of such times through the house warning system.
5. Checking to see that all fire and safety laws are obeyed.
6. Supervising the opening and closing of the house, lobby, and other public areas before and after the performance.

The house manager is present to serve the public in a very direct and immediate manner. If the musical is excellent, the publicity effective, the box office selling large quantities of tickets, and yet the audience is uncomfortable for some reason, the experience is not a complete success. If the temperature in the theatre is too hot or too cold, the restrooms are not clean, the ushers are unfriendly, or the show is twenty minutes late starting, the audience is not going to have a very good time.

The house manager may need to instruct the front-of-house staff to be courteous, efficient, and friendly. Their attitude is contagious and has a very real effect on the audience. The ushers should also be familiar with the theatre. Nothing is more embarrassing for the house manager than to have to move a row of patrons, seated mistakenly in one part of the house, to another section. A sufficient number of ushers should be used to insure a steady, even flow of customers to seats.

The house manager needs to be knowledgeable regarding the theatre's policy on latecomers. Some shows demand waiting until an appropriate break in the action; some theatres may seat latecomers at any time; still others may refuse, often because of the production itself, to seat any latecomers.

The house manager should at all times follow front-of-house protocol: never shouting or running during a performance, even in case of emergency; never using the house as an access to the backstage area; and never allowing performers or backstage personnel to loiter in the lobby area before or during the show.

Finally, the house manager needs to be prepared for the worst of all possible emergencies. In the case of fire or a fire alarm, the situation needs to be handled in a cool and organized fashion. If it is necessary to clear the house, the stage manager, performers, or house manager should make a simple, direct request for the audience to move quickly and quietly to leave the theatre. The house staff must be prepared for this type of emergency, knowing which doors to open and how to handle handicapped people or patrons with difficulty moving quickly. Preparedness is its own reward. A smooth-running front-of-house operation will not only assure the comfort and enjoyment of the audience but save wear and tear on the nerves of the house manager.

CONCLUSION

The previous discussion is some indication of the tasks facing the producer in a theatrical organization in which he or she does several jobs. Even if personnel are available to cover the areas of box office, publicity, and front of house, the producer must function as general supervisor over all personnel. Producing a musical is a large undertaking, one that will try the patience and creativity of the most energetic person. Yet when the curtain rises on opening night to a house filled with pleasant expectations, the producer realizes that his or her work has made this show possible!

PRIMARY RENTAL AGENCIES

Tams-Witmark Music Library, Incorporated
560 Lexington Avenue
New York, NY 10022

Music Theatre International, Incorporated
119 West 57th Street
New York, NY 10019

Samuel French, Incorporated
25 West 45th Street
New York, NY 10036

The Rodgers and Hammerstein Library
598 Madison Avenue
New York, NY 10022

APPENDIX B

MUSICALS RECOMMENDED
FOR PRODUCTION

Annie Get Your Gun. Lyrics and music by Irving Berlin.

Anything Goes. Lyrics and music by Cole Porter.

Applause. Music by Charles Strouse, lyrics by Lee Adams.

Apple Tree. Music by Jerry Block, lyrics by Sheldon Harnick.

Boys from Syracuse. Lyrics by Lorenz Hart, music by Richard Rodgers.

Brigadoon. Lyrics by Alan Jay Lerner, music by Frederick Loewe.

Bye Bye Birdie. Lyrics by Lee Adams, music by Charles Strouse.

Cabaret. Music by John Kander, lyrics by Fred Ebb.

Camelot. Lyrics by Alan Jay Lerner, music by Frederick Loewe.

Can-Can. Lyrics and music by Cole Porter.

Candide. Lyrics by Richard Wilbur, John Latouche, and Dorothy Parker, music by Leonard Bernstein.

Carnival! Lyrics and music by Bob Merrill.

Carousel. Lyrics by Oscar Hammerstein II, music by Richard Rodgers.

Celebration. Music by Harvey Schmidt, lyrics by Tom Jones.

Company. Lyrics and music by Stephen Sondheim.

Damn Yankees. Lyrics and music by Richard Adler and Jerry Ross.

Don't Bother Me, I Can't Cope. Lyrics and music by Micki Grant.

Ernest in Love. Lyrics by Anne Croswell, music by Lee Pockriss.

Fanny. Lyrics and music by Harold Rome.

Fantasticks. Lyrics by Tom Jones, music by Harvey Schmidt.

Fiddler on the Roof. Lyrics by Sheldon Harnick, music by Jerry Bock.

Fiorello! Lyrics by Sheldon Harnick, music by Jerry Bock.

Follies. Lyrics and music by Stephen Sondheim.

Funny Girl. Lyrics by Bob Merrill, music by Jule Styne.

A Funny Thing Happened on the Way to the Forum. Lyrics and music by Stephen Sondheim.

Girl Crazy. Lyrics by Ira Gershwin, music by George Gershwin.

Godspell. Lyrics and music by Stephen Schwartz.

Golden Boy. Lyrics by Lee Adams, music by Charles Strouse.

Grease. Lyrics and music by Jim Jacobs and Warren Casey.

Guys and Dolls. Lyrics and music by Frank Loesser.

Gypsy. Lyrics by Stephen Sondheim, music by Jule Stein.

Hair. Lyrics and music by Gerome Ragni and James Rado.

Hello, Dolly! Lyrics and music by Jerry Herman.

How to Succeed in Business Without Really Trying. Lyrics and music by Frank Loesser.

The King and I. Lyrics by Oscar Hammerstein II, music by Richard Rodgers.

Kismet. Music and lyrics by Robert Wright and George Forrest.

Kiss Me, Kate. Lyrics and music by Cole Porter.

Li'l Abner. Lyrics by Johnny Mercer, music by Gene de Paul.

Little Mary Sunshine. Lyrics and music by Rick Besoyan.

A Little Night Music. Lyrics and music by Stephen Sondheim.

Mame. Music and lyrics by Jerry Herman.

Man of La Mancha. Lyrics by Joe Darien, music by Mitch Leigh.

The Me Nobody Knows. Music by Gary William Friedman, lyrics by Will Holt.

Most Happy Fella. Lyrics and music by Frank Loesser.

The Music Man. Lyrics and music by Meredith Willson.

My Fair Lady. Lyrics by Alan Jay Lerner, music by Frederick Loewe.

New Girl in Town. Lyrics and music by Bob Merrill.

No, No, Nanette. Music by Vincent Youmans, lyrics by Irving Caesar and Otto Harbach.

Of Thee I Sing. Lyrics by Ira Gershwin, music by George Gershwin.

Oklahoma! Lyrics by Oscar Hammerstein II, music by Richard Rodgers.

On a Clear Day You Can See Forever. Lyrics by Alan Jay Lerner, music by Burton Lane.

Once Upon a Mattress. Lyrics by Marshall Barer, music by Mary Rodgers.

Paint Your Wagon. Lyrics by Alan Jay Lerner, music by Frederick Loewe.

The Pajama Game. Lyrics and music by Richard Adler and Jerry Ross.

Pal Joey. Lyrics by Lorenz Hart, music by Richard Rodgers.

Peter Pan. Lyrics by Carolyn Leigh, Betty Comden, and Adolph Green, music by Mark Charlap and Jule Styne.

Porgy and Bess. Lyrics by Ira Gershwin, music by George Gershwin.

The Prince and the Pauper. Lyrics by Verna Tomasson, music by George Fischoff.

Promises, Promises. Music by Burt Bacharach, lyrics by Hal David.

Raisin. Music by Judd Woldin, lyrics by Robert Brittan.

Seesaw. Music by Cy Coleman, lyrics by Dorothy Fields.

1776. Music and lyrics by Sherman Edwards.

Showboat. Lyrics by Oscar Hammerstein II, music by Jerome Kern.

Show Girl. Lyrics and music by Charles Gaynor.

The Sound of Music. Lyrics by Oscar Hammerstein II, music by Richard Rodgers.

South Pacific. Lyrics by Oscar Hammerstein II, music by Richard Rodgers.

The Student Prince. Lyrics by Dorothy Donnelly, music by Sigmund Romberg.

Sugar. Music by Jule Styne, lyrics by Bob Merrill.

Superman. Music by Charles Strouse, lyrics by Lee Adams.

Sweet Charity. Lyrics by Dorothy Fields, music by Cy Coleman.

Two by Two. Music by Richard Rodgers, lyrics by Martin Charnin.

Two Gentlemen of Verona. Music by Galt MacDermot, lyrics by John Guare.

The Unsinkable Molly Brown. Lyrics and music by Meredith Willson.

West Side Story. Lyrics by Stephen Sondheim, music by Leonard Bernstein.

You're a Good Man, Charlie Brown. Lyrics and music by Clark Gesner.

Zorba. Music by John Kander, lyrics by Fred Ebb.

APPENDIX C

CHRONOLOGY OF MUSICALS 1970-1988

1970
  Unfair to Goliath
  The Last Sweet Days of Isaac
  Joy
  Gantry
  Georgy
  Billy Noname
  Show Me Where the Good Times Are
  Operation Sidewinder
  Purlie
  Minnie's Boys
  Look to the Lilies
  Applause

Cry for Us All
Park
Mod Donna
Company
Colette
The Rothschilds
Sensations
The President's Daughter
Touch
Two by Two
The Me Nobody Knows
Lovely Ladies, Kind Gentlemen

1971
Stag Movie
Soon
Ari
Follies
Six
70 Girls, 70
Frank Merriwell, or Honor Challenged
The Ballad of Johnny Pot
Earl of Ruston
Godspell
Leaves of Grass
Jesus Christ Superstar
Ain't Supposed to Die a Natural Death
To Live Another Summer
The Grass Harp
Love Me, Love My Children
Twigs
Two Gentlemen of Verona
Wild and Wonderful
Inner City
Anne of Green Gables

1972
Wanted
Grease
The Selling of the President
Sugar
Don't Bother Me, I Can't Cope
Different Times
Don't Play Us Cheap
Heathen

Joan
Dude
Hurry, Harry
Pippin
Ambassador
Lysistrata
Doctor Selavy's Magic Theatre
The Contrast
Via Galactica
The Bar That Never Closes
Rainbow

1973
Shelter
A Little Night Music
Seesaw
The Karl Marx Play
Cyrano
Smith
Raisin
Molly
Gigi
More Than You Deserve

1974
Let My People Come
Lorelei
Rainbow Jones
Fashion
Sextet
Over Here!
Ride the Winds
The Magic Show
Mack and Mabel

1975
The Wiz
Shenandoah
Diamond Studs
Lovers
Man on the Moon
The Night That Made America Famous
Goodtime Charley
The Rocky Horror Show
The Lieutenant

1975 (cont'd)
Doctor Jazz
Be Kind to People Week
Philemon
Chicago
A Chorus Line
Boy Meets Boy
The Robber Bridegroom
Treemonisha
Tuscaloosa's Calling Me But I'm Not Going!
Gift of the Magi

1976
Home Sweet Homer
Pacific Overtures
Rockabye Hamlet
Rex
So Long, 174th Street
1600 Pennsylvania Avenue
Something's Afoot
Greenwich Village Follies
Don't Step on My Olive Branch
Music Is

1977
Nightclub Cantata
Starting Here, Starting Now
Movie Buff
On the Lock-In
I Love My Wife
Annie
New York City Street Show
Happy End
Love! Love! Love!
Hot Grog
The Act
Green Pond

1978
On the Twentieth Century
A Bistro Car on the CNR
A History of the American Film
The Best Little Whorehouse in Texas
Angel

Rosa
Runaways
Working
Piano Bar
I'm Getting My Act Together and
    Taking It on the Road
The Coolest Cat in Town
King of Hearts
Platinum
Ballroom
A Broadway Musical

1979
The Grand Tour
My Old Friends
They're Playing Our Song
Sarava
Sweeney Todd
A Day in Hollywood, a Night in the Ukraine
Carmelina
Dispatches
The Utter Glory of Morrissey Hall
I Remember Mama
Miss Truth
Sky High
But Never Jam Today
Evita
Sugar Babies
Potholes
God Bless You, Mr. Rosewater
Comin' Uptown

1980
Fortune
Barnum
Musical Chairs
It's So Nice to Be Civilized
Jazzbo Brown
Charlie and Algernon
Girls, Girls, Girls
Fifth of July
Ka-Boom
Trixie True Teen Detective
Alice in Concert
Onward Victoria

1981

An Evening With Joan Crawford
Real Life Funnies
In Trousers
Bring Back Birdie
Marry Me a Little
Broadway Follies
Maybe I'm Doing It Wrong
March of the Falsettos
Woman of the Year
Copperfield
The Moony Shapiro Songbook
Ah, Men
I Can't Keep Running in Place
El Bravo!
Everybody's Gettin' Into the Act
The Life and Times of Nicholas Nickleby
Marlowe
Cotton Patch Gospel
Oh, Brother
Merrily We Roll Along
The First
Tomfoolery
Head Over Heels
Dreamgirls

1982

Waltz of the Stork
Francis
Joseph and the Amazing Technicolor Dreamcoat
Pump Boys and Dinettes
Lullabye and Goodnight
I Take These Women
The Evangelist
Bags
Is There Life After High School?
Nine
Little Shop of Horrors
Do Patent Leather Shoes Really Reflect Up?
Seven Brides for Seven Brothers
Charlotte Sweet
A Doll's Life

Cats
Upstairs at O'Neal's
Foxfire
Portrait of Jennie
Snoopy

1983

Merlin
Dance a Little Closer
On the Swing Shift
Taking My Turn
Preppies
La Cage aux Folles
The Brooklyn Bridge
Up from Paradise
Tallulah
Amen Corner
Blue Plate Special
Marilyn
Doonesbury
Baby
Peg
Lenny and the Heartbreakers

1984

Sunday in the Park with George
Oliver!
Shidey MacLaure
The Human Comedy
The Tap Dance Kid
Quilters
The Three Musketeers

1985

Take Me Along
Harrigan 'n' Hart
Grind
Leader of the Pack
Big River
Singin' in the Rain
Song & Dance

1986
  Nunsense
  Me and My Girl
  Mystery of Edwin Drood
  Singing in the Rain
  Song and Dance

1987
  Starlight Express
  Les Miserables
  Into the Woods

1988
  Phantom of the Opera
  Sarafina
  Carrie
  Chess

BIBLIOGRAPHY

General Reading

Archer, Stephen. *How Theatre Happens*. (New York: Macmillan, 1977).

Balk, Wesley. *The Complete Singer-Actor* (Minneapolis: University of Minnesota Press, 1977).

Engel, Lehman. *Getting Started in the Theatre*. (New York: Collier Books, 1973).

————. *The American Musical Theatre*. (New York: Collier Books, 1975).

————. *Words With Music* (New York: Schirmer Books, 1980).

Lewine, Richard and Alfred Simon. *Songs of the Theatre* (New York: H.W. Wilson Co., 1984).

Mander, Raymond and Joe Mitchenson. *Musical Comedy: A Story in Pictures* (New York: Taplinger, 1970).

Shurtleff, Michael. *Audition* (New York: Walker, 1978).

Silver, Fred. *Auditioning for the Musical Theatre* (New York: Newmarket Press, 1985).

Acting

Benson, Herbert. *The Relaxation Response* (New York: Avon, 1976).

Berry, Cicely. *Voice and the Actor* (New York: Macmillan, 1973).

Cohen, Robert. *Acting Power* (Palo Alto: Mayfield, 1978).

Delgado, Ramon. *Acting With Both Sides of Your Brain* (New York: Holt, Rinehart, and Winston, 1986).

Gutwirth, Samuel. *You Can Learn to Relax* (Hollywood; Wilshire Book Co., 1972).

Hagen, Uta. *Respect for Acting* (New York: Macmillan, 1973).

Kosarin, Oscar. *The Singing Actor* (Englewood Cliffs: Prentice-Hall, 1983).

Linklater, Kristin. *Freeing the Natural Voice* (New York: Drama Book Publishers, 1976).

Machlin, Evangeline. *Speech for the Stage* (New York: Theatre Arts Books, 1970).

Ratliff, Gerald Lee. *Combating Stagefright* (New York: Rosen Press, 1984).

Spolin, Viola. *Improvisation for the Theatre* (Evanston: Northwestern University Press, 1963).

Directing/Producing

Cavanaugh, Jim. *Organization and Management of the Non-Professional Theatre* (New York: Rosen Press, 1973).

Clurman, Harold. *On Directing* (New York: Collier Books, 1974).

Cohen, Robert and John Harrop. *Creative Play Direction* (Englewood Cliffs: Prentice-Hall, 1974).

Davis, Christopher. *The Producer* (New York: Harper and Row, 1972).

Dean, Alexander and Lawrence Carra. *Fundamentals of Play Directing* (New York: Holt, Rinehart, and Winston, 1980).

Dolman, John. *The Art of Play Production* (New York: Harper and Brothers, 1946).

Engel, Lehman. *Planning and Producing the Musical Show* (New York: Crown, 1966).

Farber, Donald. *Producing on Broadway: A Comprehensive Guide* (New York: Drama Book Specialists, 1969).

Gregory, W.A. *The Director* (New York: Funk and Wagnalls, 1968).

Hodge, Francis. *Play Directing* (Englewood Cliffs: Prentice-Hall, 1982).

Nelms, Henning. *Play Production* (New York: Barnes and Noble, 1950).

Staub, August. *Creating Theatre: The Art of Theatrical Directing* (New York: Harper and Row, 1973).

Thomas, Bob. *Directors in Action*. (Indianapolis: Bobbs-Merrill, 1973).

Choreography/Movement

Davis, Martha. *Understanding Body Movement: An Annotated Bibliography* (New York: Arno Press, 1972).

DeMille, Agnes. *Speak to Me, Dance With Me* (Boston: Popular Library, 1973).

Fenton, Jack. *Practical Movement Control* (Boston: Plays, Inc., 1973).

Humphrey, Doris. *The Art of Making Dances* (New York: Grove Press, 1950).

King, Nancy. *A Movement Approach to Acting* (Englewood Cliffs: Prentice-Hall, 1981).

Laban, Rudolf. *The Mastery of Movement* (Boston: Plays, 1974).

Moshe, Feldenkrais. *Awareness Through Movement* (New York: Harper and Row, 1972).

Penrod, James. *Movement for the Performing Artist* (Palo Alto: National Press Books, 1974).

Oxenford, Lyn. *Design for Movement: A Textbook for Stage Movement* (New York: Theatre Arts Books, 1951).

Shawn, Ted. *Every Little Movement* (Brooklyn: Dance Horizons, 1968).

White, Edwin and Marguerite Battye. *Acting and Stage Movement* (New York: Arno Press, 1978).

Scenery/Costumes

Barton, Lucy. *Appreciating Costume* (London: Pitman and Sons, 1966).

Bay, Howard. *Stage Design* (New York: Drama Book Specialists, 1978).

Boyle, Walden and John Jones. *Central and Flexible Staging* (Berkley: University of California Press, 1956).

Burris-Meyer, Harold and Edward Cole. *Scenery for the Theatre* (Boston: Little, Brown, 1972).

Corson, Richard. *Stage Make-Up* (New York: Appleton-Century-Crofts, 1960).

Fuerst, Walter and Samuel Hume. *Twentieth-Century Stage Decoration* (New York: Benjamin Blom Inc., 1967).

Gilette, Arnold. *Stage Scenery: Its Construction and Rigging* (New York: Harper and Brothers, 1959).

Graves, Maitland. *The Art of Color and Design* (New York: McGraw-Hill Co., 1951).

Green, Ruth. *The Wearing of Costume* (London: Pitman and Sons, 1966).

Kohler, Carl. *A History of Costume* (New York: Dover Publications, 1963).

Laver, James. *Costume in the Theatre* (New York: Hill and Wang, 1964).

Mielziner, Jo. *Designing for Theatre: A Memoir and a Portfolio* (New York: Atheneum, 1965).

Motley, A. *Theatre Props* (New York: Drama Book Specialists, 1976).

Parker, Oren and Harvey Smith. *Scene Design and Stage Lighting* (New York: Holt, Rinehart, and Winston, 1968).

Lighting/Sound

Bellman, Willard. *Lighting the Stage: Art and Practice* (San Francisco: Chandler Publishing Co., 1974).

Burris-Meyer and Mallory Vincent. *Sound in the Theatre* (New York: Radio Magazine, 1959).

Collison, David. *Stage Sound* (New York: Drama Book Specialists, 1976).

McCandless, Stanley. *A Method of Lighting the Stage* (New York: Theatre Arts Books, 1958).

Rosenthal, Jean and Lael Wertenbaker. *The Magic of Light* (New York: Theatre Arts, 1973).

Rubin, Joel and Leland Watson. *Theatrical Lighting Practice* (New York: Theatre Arts Books, 1954).

Selden, Samuel and Hunton Sellman. *Stage Scenery and Lighting: A Handbook for Nonprofessionals* (New York: Appleton-Century-Crofts, 1959).

Wehlburg, Albert. *Theatre Lighting: An Illustrated Glossary* (New York: Drama Book Specialists, 1975).

Management

Gruver, Elbert. *The Stage Manager's Handbook* (New York: Harper and Row, 1953).

Langley, Stephen. *Theatre Management in America* (New York: DBS Publications, 1974).

Plummer, Gail. *The Business of Show Business* (New York: Harper and Row, 1953).

Sponsler, Whitney. *A Manual for High School and College Theatrical Administration* (Hollywood: American Legitimate Theatre Service, 1956).

Music

Fleming, William and Abraham Veinus. *Understanding Music: Style, Structure, and History* (New York: Holt, Rinehart, and Winston, 1958).

_____. *Great Songs of Broadway* (New York: New York Times Book Co., 1973).

Leichtentritt, Hugo. *Musical Form* (Cambridge: Harvard University Press, 1951).

Newman, Willilam. *Understanding Music: An Intro-duction to Music's Elements, Styles, and Forms* (New York: Harper and Row, 1961).

Marshall, Madeleine. *The Singer's Manual of English Diction* (New York: Schirmer, 1953).

Pavlakis, Christopher. *The American Music Hand-book* (New York: The Freepress, 1974).

_____. *The Bacharach and David Song Book* (New York: Simon & Schuster, 1971).

_____. *The Frank Loesser Song Book* (New York: Simon & Schuster, 1971).

_____. *The Rodgers and Hart Song Book* (New York: Simon and Schuster, 1977).

_____. *The Songs of Richard Rodgers* (New York: Williamson Music, 1979).

Smith, Cecil and Glenn Litton. *Musical Comedy in America* (New York: Theatre Arts Books, 1981).

INDEX